SMUTS

THE HUMANIST

A PERSONAL REMINISCENCE

By T. J. HAARHOFF

Sponsored by the South African
Institute of International Affairs

BASIL BLACKWELL
OXFORD
1970

© Basil Blackwell 1970

ISBN 0 631 12720 8

PRINTED IN GREAT BRITAIN
BY A. T. BROOME AND SON, 18 ST. CLEMENT'S, OXFORD
AND BOUND BY THE KEMP HALL BINDERY, OXFORD

FOREWORD

The South African Institute of International Affairs has sponsored this study of *Smuts, the Humanist* to mark the centenary of the birth of Jan Christiaan Smuts on 24th May, 1870. The author, Professor Theo Haarhoff, a Cape liberal of the Hofmeyr tradition, was a friend and confidant of Smuts, and pays tribute to his *humanitas* and political idealism. The book is not simply a defence of Smuts the politician, but a timely re-instatement of first principles, as contained in *Holism and Evolution*. Professor Haarhoff is not wide of the mark in tracing the genesis of Smuts's major work to the cultural background of the European tradition.

If not 'the noblest Roman of them all' (that title must be reserved for General Botha), Smuts was a thinker of classical stature in advance of his time. Professor Haarhoff does not set up his philosopher as a religious mystic, but he has done well to remind us that many of Smuts's ideals were misunderstood; that the neglect of their wider implications may be a tragedy for the nation he loved and helped to create. Sir Winston Churchill, speaking of Smuts in the House of Commons, said: 'He did not belong to any single state or nation. He fought for his own country; he thought for the whole world.'

The author and the Institute are greatly indebted to Professor A. C. Partridge for his generous advice and assistance in preparing this work for publication. It is appropriate, therefore, to recall a remark which Smuts once made to Professor Partridge. With his wide interests, including a love of Shakespeare, Smuts said that he saw

Shakespeare as the mouthpiece of a spiritual revolution, appealing for justice to humanity; he thought that the pleader had burnt himself out in its cause. This is largely true of Smuts himself.

Leif Egeland

Chairman of the Institute.

CONTENTS

INTRODUCTION

This book considers the fundamental thoughts of General Smuts and his ultimate aim for South Africa. Much of his thinking was not practicable in the immediate future, but it expressed his belief that South Africa should develop as part of the basic wholeness of human life. There would be many frustrations and moments of despair; but he maintained his faith in the purposive nature of life, despite all set-backs. 'On earth the broken arcs, in heaven a perfect round,' one of the many credos of Browning, was also his. This faith is now regarded with understandable scepticism; but it is a belief that Smuts never really gave up. The values that went deepest in his thinking are different from the ingenuities of the party-game; they are values possibly derived from his association with Oxford friends, and their quality is a vision that looks beyond immediate possibilities.

The group of friends that discussed the development of South Africa in student days was nurtured by the old South African College and included J. H. Hofmeyr, chosen by Smuts for his intellectual brilliance. Some went later (just before the first World War) to study in Berlin; German colleagues in our studies were Ulrich von Wilamowitz-Moellendorf and Eduard Norden. There were also P. J. du Toit of Onderstepoort and philosophers Reinhard Kottich and Raymond Willcocks, later Rector of the University of Stellenbosch, who played an important part in the development of our attitude to South Africa. To Kottich I later addressed *Briewe aan Reinhard*.

In the historical Government Avenue still stands our

old College, prototype of the University of Cape Town; the old Egyptian Building and the old lecture rooms, English with Johnnie Clark, Latin with Bill Ritchie, and P. J. du Toit for Nederlands. No Afrikaans in those days, but plenty of discussions about Afrikaans in the Debating Society; Danie Steyn was its great protagonist, a friend with the saving grace of humour. Castor and Pollux, the lions, still recline on the walls opposite the entrance gates, but gone is the old oak-tree on which hung the bell that was faithfully rung by Browne, the Janitor.

Now, as we go down the Avenue, more than fifty years later, there is the statue of General Smuts. To me it is not the man I knew. One understands artistic distortion, but the distortion must have a meaning; the aspect here is not typical of Oom Jannie, because it has no artistic meaning. The figure we knew in health was sprightly, both physically and mentally. As men stood at the steps to his office in Parliament Street, waiting for the lift, I remember that he would pass and bound up the stairs like a springbok, vivid and swift. He was then over seventy.

During the first World War there were tea-parties at the Savoy in London, which were often delightful. Sometimes the Gilletts were there and Jessie Kilburn Davis, a Quaker like the Gilletts, and my future wife. At a time when everybody seized on cakes as a special luxury, one noticed that Smuts ate nothing at all. In London bombs were falling, during air-raids, almost every evening; in Bloomsbury where I lodged people regularly took shelter in basements. I once collected a fragment of shrapnel from the vicinity. But Smuts used to go up on to the roof of the Savoy, all by himself, to watch the bombing.

He spoke to some of us about the war and South Africa. At the time things were not going too well in the war and he said that his military colleagues in London often needed cheering up. 'As hul ore begin hang, vertel ek hulle van my noue ontkomings in die Suid-Afrikaanse oorlog.' (When their ears start drooping, I tell of my narrow escapes in the South African war.) I remember a Dingaan's Day dinner (we still called it so then) in 1918, when I had to preside and Smuts sat on my right, with Olive Schreiner on my left. The air was full of hope for the proposed League of Nations, and Oom Jannie had a good deal to say about that. But Olive Schreiner shook her head. 'No, Jannie,' she said, 'not until you change human nature.' She saw further than the politicians. Gilbert Murray, scholar, artist and poet, who gets less than his due today, rightly applied his study of the Classics to the cause of *humanitas*, and worked hard with Smuts to realise the League ideal. He too was disappointed.

Those who see Smuts only as the party-politician of the newspapers grasp only a poor fragment of his richly developed personality. By temperament, he was concerned with the Greek ideal of Kosmos, an ordered world of nations. The niggling details of party politics he regarded as a necessary but boring evil. I have seen him puff out his cheeks in Parliament at some small-minded argument. It was always the ideal that illuminated his troubled activities; it was as an idealist that he stood out in contrast to most of his colleagues at the peace conference in Versailles. There he and Botha opposed the short-sighted vindictiveness that brought a violent reaction in time to come.

There were always big questions; but the smaller ones

of party politics were not shirked. His abundant vitality dealt with them; for he saw them as part of the cosmic problem and sought to give them a place in the solution of the whole.

> God gave all men all earth to live
> But, since our hearts are small,
> Ordained for each one spot should prove
> Belovèd over all.

So wrote Kipling. And Horace said of one of his favourite Italian sites:

> 'ille terrarum mihi praeter omnes . . .
> That little nook beyond all else on earth
> Has smiles for me.'

Our hearts are proverbially small. We only take in particular points of experience.

Gilbert Murray (friend and fellow-worker of Oom Jannie) shared Smuts's chief concern, the application of human values to this troubled world. The smaller things tend to prevail because they are more easily understood by the masses.

'This low man with a little thing to do' (writes Browning)
> 'Sees it and does it,
> That high man with a great thing to pursue
> Dies ere he knows it,
> That low man goes on adding one to one,
> His hundred's soon hit;
> That high man aiming at a million
> Misses an unit.'

There was an omniscient guide, showing tourists round Rome, who once boomed pompously:

'Ladies and Gentlemen, you have seen everywhere on municipal buildings the letters S.P.Q.R. and you may have been wondering what they stand for. I will tell you they mean—'

Here the voice of Gideon Roos broke in:
        'Small profits, quick returns.'

(The letters, of course, stand for *Senatus Populusque Romanus*.)
        Quick returns can be disastrous.

Browning again:
        'Oh, if we draw a circle premature
            Heedless of far gain,
        Greedy of quick returns of profit, sure
            Bad is our bargain.'

The man of vision may miss the obstacle in front of him that trips him up; but in the long run, he is the man remembered, not the clever one of quick returns. Smuts was a man of vision, a man who tried to realise the Whole.

Oom Jannie shared with the Gilletts, Alice Clark and Emily Hobhouse the truth of a world beyond our reach, beyond what is regarded by 'practical' men as the only true world.

Certain critics have said that Smuts was a lover of war. Hancock (*Smuts* I.107) says rightly that 'he always looked on war as an interruption of life's proper business'. During the Paris conference he wrote (*Hancock* I. 534): 'The League of Nations is the only bright spot in a situation of unrelieved gloom.' Yet 'I have a quiet but fundamental faith in God.' To that remarkable woman, Alice Clark, the sister of Margaret Gillett, he wrote towards the close of the First World War: 'I believe there is creative power in intense longing or praying.'

These and similar words are deeply grounded in Smuts's thought. They represent convictions that persisted in spite of great and repeated disappointments. In trying to apply the ideal truth, he was frequently frustrated by the blindness, vindictiveness and selfishness of fellow statesmen.

The Animal called Man is a difficult creature and runs mostly in blinkers.

———

'What a pity,' the old lady said at the meeting, 'that General Smuts never learned to spell. He has written a book about Holism not realising that the word *whole* begins with a *w*.' But General Smuts knew Greek and was aware that Holism came from a Greek word in which the *o* was short, as in the first syllable of Rollo. He always pronounced it short. On the fly-leaf of the second edition of *Holism and Evolution* he scribbled:

> 'To see a world in a grain of sand
> And a heaven in a wild flower—
> Hold infinity in the palm of your hand
> And eternity in an hour.'

These lines do not come from Browning, as some have thought, but from William Blake's 'Auguries of Innocence'. Matthew Arnold's 'Stanzas from the Grande Chartreuse':

> '. . . two worlds, one dead,
> The other powerless to be born';

reflect the uncertainty that Smuts felt in the complex national problems of his time. (Quoted by J. C. Smuts in the Life of his father, p. 287.)

Smuts used Holism in the sense of parts of Nature striving to become wholes. We propose to use it for the integrating factor, usually frustrated in human circumstances, that renders certain aspects of education complete and virile, only when they are combined into a significant unity. Here lies the quality in a man, be his learning ever so humble, that prompts him to keep the windows of his spirit open, to avoid the darkness of ignorant isolation or of priggish pedantry.

There is no attempt here to give a final answer to the problems of scientific principles. All that is attempted is to understand the beliefs that Smuts held, rightly or wrongly, particularly with regard to the philosophy of the whole, its origins and its possibilities.

The account is based not only on the published documents, but on many conversations with Oom Jannie and letters exchanged with him.

In this book we are trying to assess values. The politician is concerned with external power; our aim is to consider the inner force of character.

This inner force of Smuts prevailed again and again over circumstances threatening to engulf him. It constitutes for us the real Smuts, the statesman that will live in history when all the minor issues have become meaningless.

In the writing of this book I had help and encouragement from a large number of people. I can mention only a few: there was John Barratt, always ready with practical help, there was Leif Egeland so resourceful and helpful, there was the excellent Professor A. C. Partridge of the Witwatersrand University, there was Blackwell's reader, always helpful, and many others; but above all Sir Basil Blackwell, my lifelong friend and publisher.

CHAPTER I

FUNDAMENTAL UNITY IN THE WORK OF JAN CHRISTIAAN SMUTS

Looking at General Smuts's political career as a whole, we may say that he finally rejected British Imperialism, but had to express his views tentatively, step by step. He also rejected German Imperialism. Here no steps were needed. What he wanted most was the unity of Southern Africa, including Rhodesia—a task obviously for the distant future.

Behind all the party politics can be discerned a unifying factor, taking many shapes; but essentially it was the holistic principle in the mind of Jan Christiaan Smuts, though this was refuted by his political opponents.

There are two aspects of Smuts's personality that appear to be partly in conflict. On the one hand there is the lonely Stellenbosch student who, by sheer intellectual ability, won the highest distinctions in England—step by step. He was an Afrikaner with the natural reactions of a son of the veld, but with a flair for hard work and for using the opportunities presented in the interest of South Africa. He, and much less General Louis Botha, never became fully-fledged Englishmen; at the end of his life he felt it a release to return to Isie and the family at Doornkloof. His sympathy with the cause of England was condemned by many of his own countrymen; but he believed that his services to Britain would help South Africa, and this belief was largely justified. This was not opportunism. He honestly preferred British principles to the German; but he believed still more in South African unity. Milner, with his German background, generally opposed Smuts. But when the Boer leaders went to Germany after the South African War, they were coldly received.

On the other hand, there was the mighty British Empire, with its enormous prestige, extending a hand of welcome—partly in its own interests—to a young Boer who had fought against England. What a heaven-sent opportunity that was for the young Boer! President Kruger had had the insight to employ Smuts, and Smuts was loyal to him. He shared the President's attitude to British Imperialism and reacted sharply to the political manoeuvres connected with it. He felt deeply for Kruger and threw himself whole-heartedly into the struggle. He initiated and brilliantly conducted the invasion of the Cape towards the end of the war. But when, after a surprisingly long struggle against the might of Britain, the Boers had to give in, he had the foresight to see that the most profitable way for the Republic, in the interests of greater South Africa, was to co-operate, even to fighting against German Imperialism in the field.

Many utterances read as if Smuts had been converted to British Imperialism, but he was genuine in opposing the Germans. He looked ahead to the time when the help given would be a benefit to South Africa by increasing her status. He looked also at the Allies and saw beyond their idealistic talk that each was working for its own advancement. He sympathised with the moral aspirations of his Quaker friends, the Gilletts of Oxford, but also appreciated the hard facts of politics.

In spite of his long absences from home, Smuts put South Africa first. 'South Africa my first love, my only love', were the actual words he used to me. I shall never forget the sincerity with which they were spoken. They are, indeed, the unifying force in the political career of Smuts. But there was also the Smuts who loved adventure, and had the courage to face it, as he did in his invasion of the Cape Colony.

Smuts's philosophy of holism, on its political side, was particularly applicable to Southern Africa. He believed that the lower part of the continent could best be administered by the people who actually lived there; and that belief would have been feasible if it had proved elastic enough to admit of modification in the light of experiences. Smuts would have liked to include Rhodesia, and he made two efforts to persuade her leaders. Many Rhodesians today are sorry that they did not listen to him. But he had no ambitions beyond stability; his cause was not on the same footing as 'the scramble for Africa'.

But a difference arose in regard to the non-whites. Here Smuts held the traditional Afrikaner view. He was kindly in his attitude. Overseas he sat by many distinguished non-whites and had good friends among them. But in the South African context he supported the tradition of separate development, and insisted that in the circumstances it was the only practicable policy. For reasons of practical politics he never adopted the views of British liberals on matters like the franchise. But he did not favour laws that were to stand for all time: there was always to be an element of elasticity. If he had lived today, with his keen awareness of world conditions, he would have modified his views in the direction of liberalism. He was a practical politician, accustomed to estimate the course to be followed in a particular situation at a particular time, but he always tried to avoid dogmatic pronouncements.

Holism, therefore, was limited for Smuts politically by the circumstances of the situation in South Africa. But in shared ideals there were no such limits. His letters to friends in Oxford, as we shall see, show this clearly, especially the letters to Alice Clark. Her world of spiritual values was very real to him, and genuine. He understood that the philosophy of the whole would remain unrealised, because it was perhaps unrealisable. But it was something to aim at, a light to give direction; fraught with frustration, but deeply embedded, as a hope for the future, in the nature of the Universe.

The result of some irreconcilable relationships is that Smuts's reputation in Europe has suffered, largely in the minds of people, in themselves admirable, who judge by abstract principles, but cannot appreciate the difficulties of a practical statesman in a country like South Africa. Smuts's job, after all, was to do what was possible in a particular society with particular people, and we should try to respect his judgment. He was prepared to modify existing arrangements in the liberal direction, when he saw an opportunity. Dogmatism on ultimate principles, he foresaw, as the political danger; the rigid mind, in this changing world, does not lead to wisdom. But unfortunately the mind that is prepared, with wisdom, to adapt itself to the future, drives the extremists into a panic. The achievement of a balanced outlook is difficult here, because it invariably exposes people to distrust and criticism; but that outlook was the aim of J. C. Smuts, and the extent to which he achieved it is his title to fame.

Perhaps an observation may be interpolated here. His second name often appears as Christian, with one *a*. This is an Anglicised form. The baptismal register shows Christiaan, with two *a*'s, as Hancock has pointed out. But in a bilingual country custom establishes different modes of spelling, and there is no doubt that Christian, with one *a*, was widely used. *Si volet usus*, as Horace said: 'if custom so decrees, custom has the rule of speech in its power.'

Let us look at the man Smuts, and try to establish the background of his complex personality, his conduct of affairs in general, and his special South African attributes. There will be no need to introduce the minutiae of local politics, though their relation to his public work cannot be ignored.

Chapter II

SMUTS THE GREEK

Oom Jannie first met Greek studies during a six-day holiday before his final term at Stellenbosch. He locked himself in his room and mastered Greek to such an extent that he headed the Cape lists in this subject. He could memorize much in his prescribed books merely by reading them through. When friends and I walked through the Ashmolean Museum at Oxford, looking at Greek statues, somebody said: 'Why, look, there is General Smuts!' It was a statue of Demosthenes, after the work of Polyeuktos from Hellenistic times, and it certainly seemed to bear a resemblance to Smuts.

Smuts was a Greek. He was always attracted by Greek philosophy. He liked the modern Greeks, and they got on well with him. A street in Athens was once called after him; but the Athenians keep changing their street names, so it is not there today. His fondness for Princess Frederika, who often came to the home in Doornkloof with her family, and loved it in spite of its cold and chaos, was deep and genuine; but it was distorted by scandal-loving journalists. Smuts wrote about her: 'A shrewd and able good woman, in addition to being a German'. (She was, in fact, a grand-daughter of Kaiser Wilhelm II.) 'It was clear that she was a real good German who hated Hitler and all his works and thoughts, and longed for a peace which would finish Nazism, but spare her people.... I could make good use of the great parable of the Sower and the sparing of the tares for the sake of the wheat,

6

which I said embodied not only the essence of Christianity, but also of Greek philosophy, which throughout is based on the idea of not going to the limit, not overstepping the bounds of moderation and fairness, and following the idea of the Whole. *Sophrosyne* is Greek for both moderation and wisdom. This brought us to Holism. . . .' So wrote Smuts of a conversation he had with her.

To Holism Princess Frederika became an enthusiastic convert, and so established a spiritual bond with Smuts. They had many discussions on philosophy. Hancock notes: 'Smuts from 1942 onwards devoted a disproportionate amount of his time to Greek affairs'. But there is no doubt that, quite apart from Princess Frederika, Smuts was genuinely interested in Greece and attracted to its history, which influenced his work on world peace. His speeches on democracy have much in common with those of Pericles, whose idealism he shared. He visited Greece as often as circumstances allowed.

He always practised Greek simplicity and nearness to Nature, which characterised the Roman farmer as well. When I was asked for an inscription to be engraved on the Smuts plaque at the Wilds in Johannesburg, I decided on a line from Vergil's Georgics, *fortunatus et ille, deos qui novit agrestes*—'blessed also is he who knows the gods of the countryside'. Lucretius was blest because he had an intellectual understanding of Nature. So did Smuts. But Vergil, like Smuts, had also the living practical experience of Nature. To Oom Jannie Table Mountain was a cathedral where he heard a subtler music, saw wider visions, and was inspired by a loftier spirit. He declined luxury, especially if it could not be shared with others. When, after the Second World War, he was sent during the peace negotiations to Eastern Europe and saw the want and starving in those parts, he refused the sumptuous dinner that had been prepared for him, and lived on army rations of the simplest kind.

We know that Smuts, in 1937, turned again to the New Testament in its original Greek version. Hancock (*Smuts* II. *The Fields of Force*, p. 305) quotes from a letter of 3 April, 1937: 'I have recently taken to reading the New Testament again in Greek, partly to recover some of my half-forgotten Greek but especially to see whether I can now get some fresh light on the Gospel story. . . . We have put such a thick varnish of glosses and interpretations on the original account that a special effort has to be made to get back the simple intention of the original authors. So I am once more re-reading the wonderful story and have now done most of Matthew. . . . When I last read the Greek Testament, it was with very orthodox eyes, which I have no longer. And yet I am probably today more interested to get at its meaning than I was in my orthodox youth.'

One morning at breakfast the Oubaas quoted a verse from I Corinthians 13, and Ouma thereupon recited the whole glorious chapter in the original Greek (*Hancock*, Smuts II. 342; *Letters* vol. 63 No. 85, to M. C. Gillett). Isie was devoted to Greek drama and shared the Oubaas's enthusiasm for Greek literature and culture. Oom Jannie attached great importance to the words of Jesus: 'The Kingdom of God is within you.' As he studied the New Testament, he asked the question: 'How does it translate into human affairs?' 'I feel the tragedy of the situation,' he wrote to his Quaker friends, 'as deeply as any Friend' (member of the Society of Friends); 'and I do believe that under ideal conditions the Christian message is the only answer' (*Hancock*, Smuts II. p. 426). 'To me, in the deepest sense, a man like Jesus can never die, but does live on in men's souls for ever. And those very senses are made alive and resurrected by His indwelling spirit and presence'. He accepted ideas that went beyond material science. He affirmed the reality of a transcendent unseen world.

He frequently read Emily Bronte's poems in the last years of his life. They had their place with his Greek Testament on the little table beside his bed. (*Letters* Vol. 80, quoted *Hancock* II. 494). Without his Greek Testament, he said, he could scarcely have survived the war and its frustrations. It carried him from his little world not only into another little world, but into the universe (*Letters* Vol. 66, *Hancock* II. 402).

He came from a little world, a small nation. That too was a link with Greece, which had fought for freedom against immense odds, as Oom Jannie and the Boers had done. Demosthenes had championed small Athens and her freedom, and launched spirited attacks—the famous *Philippics*—against the greater Macedonia, which was destined to dominate Greece. So Smuts came forward to champion the Transvaal, and launched *The Century of Wrong*, written mainly by himself, we are told, against the enemies of his small people. Looking back later, he may have smiled at the violence of his attack. But at that time he was wholehearted and sincere. Activity of the body and of mind animated his whole being.

The Greek ideal in education was a combination of intellectual studies in various aspects, literary, artistic, philosophic (at that time philosophy included science); it went under the general title of *Mousike*, because it was thought to depend on the inspiration of the Muses. Now the Greek word *Mousa*, we are told, was originally *Montya*

9

in which the syllable *Mon-* is related to the word for *memory*. The Muses bring back memories from the sub-conscious history of the race, and what looks like a new discovery is sometimes an old truth revived by the man of genius, the man who knows the guidance of a 'guardian spirit'. The Romans called this the Genius, and it is sometimes referred to by Plato as the Daimon. Not all can respond to this guidance; indeed, only a small percentage. But culture and insight depend on the degree of response. In Smuts the response was very active and vivid. It was also swift. He retained his Greek and worked at it with Isie, his wife, using it in old age for re-reading the New Testament.

Mousike, which gives us our word music, was only one side of Greek education. The other was *Gymnastike*, the exercise of the body for which one stripped and made one's self *gymnos*, literally 'naked', but in effect lightly clad for exercise. The two things went together in the ancient Greek, also in Smuts. His devotion to work on the farm and to climbing Table Mountain, not without his famous *Alpenstock*, even when he was well over seventy, was something in which he outdid all the younger members of his Cabinet; he never succumbed to the middle-aged spread. He remained intensely active in mind as well as in body, and so fulfilled the Greek ideal of the educated man.

The modern ideal of an educated man was, to me, the Oxford Professor of Greek, Gilbert Murray, who became a friend of Smuts and worked with him on the League of Nations. To hear Gilbert Murray read a chorus ending of Euripides, in the original, was in itself an education. To hear him applying the principle of *humanitas* to the world was an inspiration; it was the final justification of Classical Studies.

With his Quaker friends in Oxford Smuts listened to readings from Gilbert Murray's translations of Greek tragedy. On his voyage back to South Africa, in 1906, these friends gave him books which included Murray's translations of Euripides's *Electra* and *The Trojan Women*. The language of Murray's translations even crept into Smuts's correspondence. For example, in 1919 he wrote to Alice Clark, the sister of Margaret Gillett, on his journey back to South Africa: 'I have spent a quiet, happy time on board . . . mostly in reflections on the past. . . . What a tremendous past it has been! Is anything still left? Will they ever come again, the long, long dances?' Here he was quoting from Murray's translation of Euripides's *Bacchae* (Vs. 862ff.)—the famous chorus in which occurs the often quoted line which Murray translated 'and shall not loveliness be loved for ever?'

Murray told Smuts that he found the word Holism etymologically correct and politically suitable, but did not like its sound. The problems of a new international order were continually in the minds of both Murray and Smuts during the First World War, and they had many discussions at the house of the Gilletts, 102 Banbury Road, where I often went for tea on Sundays. Gilbert Murray gave Smuts encouragement and support. So did the Oxford scholars J. A. Smith and A. D. Lindsay, particularly on his holistic philosophy. Smuts told Gilbert Murray that Holism (in its true sense) embodied his fundamental belief.

The traditional epithet for Odysseus among the Greeks was *polytropos*, the man who turned in many directions. The Latin in Livius Andronicus is *versutus* or *vorsutus* (*verto*, I turn). Did this refer to the mind or the physical travels of Odysseus's body? There are two schools of thought. (See *The Ulysses Theme* by W. B. Stanford, Blackwell, 1954.) I believe it meant both. It is a description both of the mind and of the physical activities of Odysseus; and it also describes the intense mental activity of J. C. Smuts. He was the Odysseus of our time. His many travels are on record; in the end he longed, like Odysseus, to see the smoke rising from his own humble dwelling, and to be at rest with Nature. But he never shirked a call when it came.

I once sat behind him while he was addressing a meeting in the City Hall, Cape Town. I noticed his hands. They were never at rest behind his back; the fingers kept twining and interweaving in rapid motion. That was the symbol of his active mind, the mind that could always 'make a plan'. It darted in many directions. The mind that stood before the Welsh audience at Tonypandy, when a strike was threatened that would have caused extreme embarrassment to the Lloyd George government in 1917. It had been decided to send Smuts to them. He was greeted with jeers and whistles. But he 'made a plan'. He told them that he did not belong to their country; but the fame of Welsh singing had reached him, and that he would like to have the privilege of hearing them. That won them over. They responded in a flash and struck up 'Land of our Fathers', the singing of which was so enthusiastic that the acrimony of dispute gave way to settlement.

Thus the Ulysses theme, as Stanford has shown, runs through history and has many aspects. We start with '*polytropos Odysseus*' and rediscover it, with modifications, in 'slim Jannie'.

The Greek, especially in 5th century Athens, was

always in search of new experience. Later St. Paul found that 'all the Athenians, and strangers which were there, spent their time in nothing else but either to tell or hear some new thing' (*Acts of the Apostles*, 17:21). This restless spirit of enquiry was typical of ancient Greeks; it was typical also of their modern counterpart, Jan Christiaan Smuts. It was Euripides who wrote about the Athenians (I quote the version of Gilbert Murray):

> They are hungered and, lo, their desire
> With wisdom is fed as with meat,
> In their skies is a shining fire
> And a joy in the fall of their feet.

Like Aeneas, Smuts was often FATO PROFUGUS, an exile of Fate, ranging without respite over many regions. In Homer, *Odyssey*, Book V, we find Odysseus sitting on a headland, his eyes full of tears, as he gazes across the sea in longing. When Hermes comes at the bidding of Zeus to tell Calypso that she must let Odysseus go, she is angry. She gives him a lavish banquet and warns of all the difficulties he will have to face. Penelope is mortal, while she, Calypso, is immortal. But he still prefers home and little Ithaca.

There is a parallel here in the persuasive voices that tried to induce Oom Jannie to become a member of the British Cabinet. His letters were full of longing for home. To take only one example, on 12.1.1906 he wrote, during a brief visit to London: 'my heart longs ardently for the precious ones away in the south of the dear fatherland'. The letter is in Dutch, with Afrikaans breaking through here and there. He refused the invitation to stay in Britain. Hancock thinks he made a mistake in accepting the 'Field-Marshal' distinction. But he still

asked to be known as 'General Smuts'. He might well
have reflected, with Tennyson's 'Ulysses':

> . . . . all times I have enjoyed
> Greatly, have suffered greatly, both with those
> That loved me and alone.
> . . . Much have I seen and known; cities of men,
> And manners, climates, councils, governments,
> Myself not least, but honoured of them all.
> . . . How dull it is to pause, to make an end,
> To rest unburnished, not to shine in use!
>
> Though much is taken, much abides; and though
> We are not now that strength which in old days
> Moved earth and heaven, that which we are, we are;
> One equal temper of heroic hearts,
> Made weak by time and fate, but strong in will
> To strive, to seek, to find and not to yield.

CHAPTER III

HERACLEITUS, PLATO AND ARISTOTLE IN SMUTS'S THINKING

The extent of Smuts's acquaintance with Greek philosophy will never be precisely known, but he must have acquired a great deal indirectly from his friendship with Gilbert Murray, A. D. Lindsay and other scholars at Oxford.

Heracleitus, who was in his prime about 500 B.C., was a native of Ionia on the West coast of Asia Minor, which saw the awakening of Greek thought and the great figure of Homer, before the illuminating period of Athens. He belongs to Ephesus, one of the famous twelve cities of Ionia which fostered the three fundamentals—search for order, search for truth and search for beauty. The inhabitants of these cities had an Asiatic element, but no race exclusiveness, such as infected some of the later Greeks, who spoke of *Barbaroi*. They were said to be the sons of Javan of Genesis 10.4.

Heracleitus was a solitary and a philosopher, critical of the Ephesian concentration on commercial interests; an aristocrat who, with royal connections, refused an invitation to the court of King Darius of Persia. He was by far the greatest figure among the thinkers of Ionia.

The Ionians began by asking the question that is still being asked: What is the ultimate element in the composition of the world we live in? They, like us, were concerned with the question 'what is life?' to which a final answer has not yet been given.

15

Heracleitus believed in the visible world and tried to solve its problems. But he also believed in an invisible world of a divine order. He believed in a plan or law for the universe, which he called its Logos.

Now this is the term used at the beginning of the Fourth Gospel, where is is (quite inadequately) translated by Word. In the beginning was the Logos—the Divine plan for the universe, with its enormous, its unlimited implications. It was universal, but men could not understand it. Heracleitus also spoke of a radiant energy as a basic element in the universe. There is apparent strife, he even calls it 'war', but the end is attunement, balance, harmony.

Heracleitus did not envisage a Creator functioning at a particular point of time. Neither did Smuts. There is a creative process going on at particular times and in particular circumstances, but not a definite and final act of creation as in the book of Genesis. The idea of creativeness, however, is accepted both by Heracleitus and by Smuts. The final stage is a return to Fire, that is, to life-energy, which marks the end of a particular life or a particular era, in the sense that it is taken up into the Whole, where it is still governed by the laws of the Logos. Its life goes on.

Shortly before he died, Dr. Robert Broom, one of our most distinguished scientists, said to me: 'I don't care what the current opinions are, I am an Aristotelian, I believe there is Design in evolution.' He denied the idea that all was simply a matter of chance. All things are filled with souls and divinities. All human laws are derived (if they are genuine!) from one divine law. We have the strife of opposites producing the whole and

16

making the universe one. This is very like the philosophy of Smuts.

Smuts realised, as Heracleitus and Plato did, that the ordinary material world was not the final truth, and that the invisible part of life is more important than the visible. The best we can attain by our own means is childish compared with the divine.

Heracleitus, one of the oldest of the Greek scientists, is also the most modern in his contact with the thoughts of J. C. Smuts. In physics he links up with Heisenberg, and in psychology with Carl Jung. Heracleitus 'discovered the most remarkable of all psychological laws, namely the regularity function of opposites' (Jacobi: *The Psychology of Jung*, p. 50). The stability of opposite tensions is now fully recognised.

In the *Timaeus* of Plato the soul of all human beings is said to be the work of the Demiourgos, who is identified with God. The account is in mythical form, but it seems to represent the fundamental philosophy of Plato.

Plato believed there was a purpose in Nature, though he might have hestitated to describe himself as a teleologist. The *telos* or end to which the universe developed, was simply a process with which Man could co-operate, if he wished. Working towards it did not imply a loss of freedom or initiative. In man there is an intelligent process of building Wholes. But there must be varying stages of achievement, and many incomplete efforts. Wholeness can be achieved only in part during our lives. But those who rise to the experience of true Wholeness for a short space have tasted a harmony that rewards them for many disappointments.

Plato insists that the universe is the product of intelligent design and beneficent purpose; and this links

17

him with modern scientists like Bruno, Whitehead, Eddington and Jeans. His vision of creative evolution divinely guided (*Kosmos*, 'order' out of chaos) is opposed to the views of materialists. Plato wrote over the entrance to his Academy, 'Let no one unversed in geometry enter here'. His explanation of the Universe was that 'God geometrises'. He discussed the many shapes and combinations of the rotary movement of the Universe, which never ceases, as Heracleitus said, yet preserves balance and stability, through the tension of opposites. Behind our world of perpetual change is a world of eternal and immutable ideas, which we can only partially grasp. We see particular forms around us, but in order to find real knowledge we need to perceive the general principle, the One, the Universal, that unites the Many, which are particular concrete examples. We should never look on the One and the Many as irreconcilable opposites, but find the links between them, see them as co-existing and complementary.

Plato, not Aristotle, laid down the essentials of the scientific spirit. They were:

(1) The researcher must have infinite patience in exploring possibilities and hypotheses.

(2) He must be uninfluenced by sentiment or self-interest.

(3) He must be entirely honest, and not try to 'cook' his results.

(4) He must have the courage 'to follow the argument whithersoever it leads', even if the result is contrary to his wishes.

With all this Smuts, the scientist-philosopher, agreed. But for any party-politician such a world view was not easy.

18

My Oxford tutor used to say that in Plato's view the educated man should not be satisfied merely with the acquisition of knowledge and professional techniques, but aim at understanding relationships, forging living links between the abstract and the practical, seeing the connection between thought and human interests, achieving perspective, explaining how a theme fits into the Whole of which it forms a part. Holism, which is Greek by etymology, is Greek also in significance; for it was Plato who first conceived the synoptic view of education.

The Platonic outlook was the parent of *humanitas*, the quality of the civilised citizen who seeks the connection between men and things. What do we mean by Humanism? The spirit that looks for significant connections; that seeks a harmony between man and men, between man and Nature, between man and God. Humanism, in Cicero and Vergil, desired a unity, as distinct from uniformity, between Rome and Italy, between Hellenic and Italian culture, between Greek science and the ancestral rustic religion of the Romans. It is a spirit instinct with sympathy, and filled with pity for the blindness of human striving; appreciative both of the humour and of the pathos of life; a spirit strong enough to be unpopular in its steadfast pursuit of the best; almost, it would seem, necessarily unpopular, because it sees humanity as a Whole, and is therefore liable to be accused of disloyalty to a particular party. Even in the pride of national victory, humanism refuses to be blinded by chauvinism. It is thus opposed to a spirit seen in Europe and in our own country today, that seeks to establish a cause by rousing the passion of hatred, and to win a victory by excluding everything that may show the other side in a favourable light; for humanism believes, in spite of everything, that truth will outlast party, and that the lie in the soul is the ultimate degradation.

Humanism, in the sense described, is the parent of Holism; the descent is lineal and direct. That the holistic tendency is becoming one of the characteristics of the present time has been asserted by many thinkers.

In Plato the form was transcendental, *outside* the world of the senses; in Aristotle there is a force (*Eidos*), *inside* the material world that gives things their validity (Lesky, p. 558; Ross, *Aristotle*, p. 126). Movement in the heavens occurs because the Universe is drawn by an attraction that Aristotle likens to love or desire.

Aristotle rejects chance in the development of natural phenomena. In *Physics* 196A he says: 'The early physicists found no place for chance among the causes which they recognised'; in 198A: 'We must explain then that nature belongs to the class of causes which act for the sake of something.'

Smuts used a similar Aristotelian terminology in *Holism and Evolution*: 'There is a process with a persistent trend (in Nature) which cannot possibly be the result of mere accident. . . . In fact the idea of Chance arises from a too limited and abstract view of the facts' (p. 185). 'The persistent direction on the whole shows that it is not self-sufficiency. It has a trend, it has a list. It has an immanent *Telos*' (p. 187).

Hancock, however, says positively (I. 306) 'There is no direct evidence that Smuts had studied Aristotle, and there is direct evidence that he had not studied Aquinas, but his thought is saturated through and through with their teleology. He did not find it incompatible with evolutionary theory.'

20

Evolution, for Smuts, was development to a plan, whatever the origin of the plan might be. The plan implied, in Smuts's view, individual effort and a long self-disciplined struggle for attainment. It was possible for Evil to increase, even as Good progressed; the spiritual struggle was like the tension of opposites in Heracleitus. He found, indeed, that as an advance was made towards an ideal, the forces of opposition often increased. Imperfect wholes seem to strive with greater intensity towards the realisation of their destiny as Wholes. One advantage of the struggle is that it gives hope and adventure to life. For this reason Smuts himself always returned to a forward-looking attitude, despite set-backs. A challenge to the fighting spirit of Oom Jannie always met a response.

In Smuts's early work 'Walt Whitman', a study in the evolution of personality, we see the beginning of his interest in Holism. Wholeness is the result of continuous development of the personality, and this needs freedom. But freedom is conditioned by circumstances, environment and inherited characteristics. It is not absolute, but subject to modification as knowledge progresses.

Hancock speaks of the holistic 'virus' which 'infected' many people, and mentions a distinguished professor of philosophy who describes Holism as 'the creed of tribalism and collectivism, a devilish totalitarian invention for the glorification of the state and the enslavement of the individual. . . . One would normally suppose that a soldier has failed when he agrees to surrender, and that a philosopher has failed when he cannot find even one person to read his book through'.

This is a sad misconception of Smuts's thought and aims, as Hancock affirms.

Smuts's interest in Holism was not just an episode; it was a life-long pursuit, deeply embedded in his being. He always wanted to revise and complete his book, which was the supreme expression of his personality.

Chapter IV

SMUTS THE ROMAN

Whether we look at the Athenians, the Spartans or the Thebans, the attempts of the unilingual Greeks to build an empire were failures. The Romans, with their sense of law, built a more abiding structure that not only made a profound impression on succeeding generations, but also saved the Greek cultural tradition for them. For the Romans, who began with antipathy, were converted to Greek civilisation when they learned the second language and became upholders of the Greek achievement. They produced a Whole from two different traditions.

At the outset the Romans were faced by enemies of different races. It was a time, as Mommsen says, when an aspiring people had to be either the hammer or the anvil. They had to survive to make their contribution, as did the Voortrekkers. The Romans were the most suitable people to emerge from the racial turmoil and guide the future development of Italy.

Smuts saw in the early Romans a resemblance to the Boers. Both were farmer-soldiers, commandeered when the need arose; the institution of a professional Roman army came later. Both were deeply attached to the family and the household gods; they knew the meaning of *pietas*, loyalty to tradition. Both were conservative and therefore afraid of foreign influence. The outlook of the Roman, with his strong sense of discipline, was Stoic; and the Stoic philosophy upheld order and obedience to recognised authority. Dean Inge actually called Calvinism, the Boer's religion, 'baptized Stoicism'.

Greek theatres, Greek doctors, Greek philosophers, Greek art and science, Greek gods, were originally regarded as dangerous importations from overseas. The old Roman had his 'huismiddels' (traditional household remedies) like the old-fashioned Afrikaner. On the other hand there was a tradition of guest-friendship (*hospitium*); strangers from Europe were generally made welcome, even though they sometimes abused the hospitality and departed with the family silver. This tradition was taken seriously and protected both by religion and law. Vergil makes Dido say that Jupiter, the highest religious power, laid down the laws for guest and host; the relationship was often recorded on a token (*tessera*), to which there is reference in inscriptions. In 394 B.C. (to take one example) a magistrate of Liparae, who protected Roman ambassadors from pirates, was granted public *hospitium* by the Senate.

In their attitude to foreigners the Romans may have had periods of exclusiveness; but on the whole, as Phillipson remarks (*International Law and Custom of Ancient Rome*), they were much more liberal than the Greeks. The Romans saw that the non-Romans, as a class, had something to contribute; the Greeks, as a rule, did not take this view of the non-Greeks, the *Barbaroi*; they excluded even the half-Greek Macedonians.

Smuts found in the Romans forceful enterprise and untiring persistence; their ability to recover reminded him of the South African plant 'Kannie-dood', which has a mysterious continuance of life. The Romans usually began by losing battles and ended by winning the war. Defeat was not the end of the story. This spirit Oom

Jannie saw in Paul Kruger, for whom he had a deep and genuine regard.

When he addressed a great crowd of Stellenbosch students, at the invitation of the Students' Representative Council, on the Coetzenburg football ground in October, 1949, the year before his death, he was accompanied by a venerable pillar of the Dutch Reformed Church, the Rev. A. F. Louw, who had been a prisoner at St. Helena. It was not a party-political meeting. All the sentiment of his early days at Stellenbosch, and his connection with President Kruger, surged up in him. The students realised the genuine emotion behind his words and responded with enthusiasm. His appreciation of the Voortrekker tradition and the character of his ancestors was centred on Paul Kruger. He gave the lie to political opponents who had summed him up as 'slim Jannie'. He was certainly not an Anglicised Imperialist. Paul Kruger, he said, had been a creative leader, a religious man who followed 'die heilige linie', the holy line that ran through human history. Hancock (*Smuts* II. 523) rightly criticises the tame translation of an English paper 'the spiritual thread'. The phrase was linked with his final conception of Holism, namely that the Whole is not complete unless it includes the values of the Greek and Roman traditions.

Smuts, then, understood the Voortrekker situation in Roman and South African history. But there was also the linguistic and cultural aspect.

The Romans, after a struggle, became bilingual, and the cultured Roman was a man of both languages (*homo utriusque linguae*) and the inheritor of two traditions. This did not mean that he neglected Roman literature, but rather that his own cultural tradition was enriched by the advent of Greek. He overcame the initial fear that he would be swamped. *Mutatis mutandis*, that was what Smuts wanted for South Africa. But it was an adjustment that would take time and needed care; and there were always people with the Romans, as with us, who wanted to upset the balance.

The Roman farmer-soldier was a pioneer whose task it was to open up the country and to ensure his place in the community of many races. Human nature being what it is, this entailed many wars, many defeats and many recoveries. There was at first little time to think of cultural development. The Roman had learned to write by the sixth Century B.C., and developed his own metre for verse. The first epic was in that metre, a translation of Homer by Andronicus, three centuries later.

So the first verses in Afrikaans were translations, and the metres were taken from English. English had the older and richer literature in South Africa, and it naturally provided models in the beginning.

The beginning of Roman literature dates from the middle of the third Century B.C., although Greeks had lived in the South of Italy from about the eighth century. Pyrrhus, looking at the primitive farmer-community on the Tiber, thought it would be a romantic excursion to go and conquer them with modern techniques and elephants. At first he carried all before him. But Roman character and perseverance prevailed in 275 B.C. A Pyrrhic victory to-day is one that is decisive in the beginning, but whose outcome recoils on the aggressor. Violence invariably ends like that.

In the first conflict with Carthage (264–241 B.C.) the Romans came into contact with the Sicilian Greeks and won military victories; but the ultimate victory was for Greek culture in Rome; 'the Greek captive took captive

26

the fierce conqueror', as Horace, the phil-Hellene, wrote later.

The decisive date for the establishment of Greek Culture was the third Century B.C. Greek customs came to be accepted, and the theatre became an interesting discovery. Politically, the Roman felt more secure after defeating the Carthaginians, who were the leading commercial power in the Mediterranean; there was more time to indulge in cultural pursuits.

So, in the old Cape Colony, English was fashionable and English culture was taken for granted. Nevertheless, there were dissentient voices. Some people in the Cape felt that their individuality was being swamped. A Roman Nationalist was a member of the older generation who was afraid of the encroaching influence of Greek. There certainly were people of that kind at the Cape and they chose a champion in S. J. du Toit of Paarl, who founded *Die Genootskap van Regte Afrikanders* in 1875 with the aim 'to stand for our language, our nation and our country.'

Movements like this have vacillating success. At Rome in the second Century B.C., Quintus Ennius came forward as the champion of the pro-Greeks. He said he had three hearts—*tria corda*—Roman, Greek and Italian, meaning by the last that he shared the sentiments of the tribes living in Italy, such as the Oscans, whose language the Romans did not suppress, and whose plays were performed in Rome as late as the time of Augustus. Ennius is said to have had a divided personality; but he was a loyal citizen of Rome, and fought in the Roman army. He could sympathise culturally with the contributions of Greeks and Italians.

This, in South Africa, was the attitude of J. C. Smuts.

His loyalty to South Africa was not impaired by his appreciation of English or German culture. Perhaps Smuts tended to neglect the Afrikaans contribution. Just as the attitude of Ennius provoked a strong Nationalist protest in the person of Marcus Porcius Cato, so the attitude of Smuts was responsible, in part, for Nationalist emphasis on 'our own literature and tradition'. Cato wanted all Hellenic influence to be eradicated and campaigned against Greek. He was a thorough-going Roman Nationalist.

There is a similarity between the Cape and the Italian landscape, which Smuts knew. John Buchan (Lord Tweedsmuir) who was well acquainted both with the Classics and the Cape, wrote in his autobiography (*Memory Hold the Door*, p. 36) 'If you seek the true classical landscape outside Italy and Greece, you will find it on the Cape Peninsula, in places like Paarl and Stellenbosch.' The Mediterranean climate of the Cape favoured agricultural customs that had parallels in ancient Italy.

It happened some years ago that a simple Boer farmer read my Afrikaans translation of the *Georgics*. He sat up, as Vergil puts it, 'by the late light of the winter fire', and learned with a surprised fellow-feeling how the Roman farmer ploughed with oxen, as he himself did; saw him leading water in furrows, according to the age-long Mediterranean custom; heard how he burned the stubble of his cornfields to fertilise them, just as he himself burned his veld; re-discovered his own practice of fallowing land and rotating crops; read about the selection of seeds, the making of hedges, the dipping of sheep (*Geo.* I. 272). Rivers that are all but dry in summer, and come down suddenly in irresistible volume, were as well known in Italy, as in the northern provinces of South

Africa. He recognised a practice of his own servants in dealing with bees that are troublesome—they can be scattered by throwing up handfuls of dust (*pulveris exigui iactu*). Then he read how the Roman farmer made his torches by the fire in winter, while his wife sang at her weaving or boiled on the fire her grape juice in a copper cauldron, removing the froth with leaves. The commentators misunderstood this practice, both in England and in France. But, of course, we have long known it as the making of *moskonfyt*, which is *mustum* (grape juice), plus *confectum*. The Romans used the product as we do, partly as a syrup and partly as a means of sweetening acid wines.

Smuts understood the background and problems of the old Roman farmer, because he knew the Boer character that was produced in similar surroundings. Brought up in a tough school, the Boer had learned, like the Roman, to endure hardness. Paul Kruger could amputate his own thumb with his clasp-knife, when it had become gangrenous from the bursting of his gun, and Gaius Mucius Scaevola could hold his hand in the fire of the Etruscan Porsenna, who had ordered him to be burned alive after his attempt on the life of the tyrant. Porsenna was so much impressed by the stoicism of Scaevola, that he freed him.

Gradually, with conservative slowness, the Roman adapted himself to the thought that it was to his advantage to profit by Greek culture, while preserving his own identity. But there were outbursts of the narrow outlook now and then, just as there are in South Africa.

In Vergil, a harmonisation was achieved that enables us to realise that the Roman of two languages and two cultures was superior to the Roman of one language and one culture. The former was a richer man, at any rate in the period when this was the accepted ideal, from 3rd Century B.C. to the 4th Century A.D. (i.e. for some six hundred years). Greek influence then moved East to Byzantium, Constantinople or Istanbul, which is a corruption of Greek *es ten polin* (to the city). The six hundred years in question produced the best type of Roman citizen. This, then, should be the answer to those who maintain that bilingualism is a weakening of the national character; that the thing to aim at is one people, one language. That certainly was not the ideal of Smuts. If it had been, he could never have gained the world recognition that came to him. He saw the two European cultures forming a Whole in South Africa, supplementing each other; and that is how Wilamowitz saw Greek and Roman culture in the ancient world. Smuts became more and more sensitive, at the same time, to the recognition of the languages and cultures of the Africans.

That was Oom Jannie's holistic view for South Africa. But destiny led him into wider fields. He was drawn to play an important part in the politics of Europe, and to be looked to for help by people who had fought against him in the South African War. The speeches he made under people like Lloyd George, and the organisations he built up in England and elsewhere in Europe, show a Roman side to Oom Jannie that England and America, under Woodrow Wilson, were glad to acknowledge. This was an ironical turn of events for the simple Boer, who had written *A Century of Wrong*, and had opposed the British Empire in the field for some three years! It is amazing to think of him swaying those enormous audiences and guiding those great figures in the British War Cabinet; of his being sent on one-man missions to win over difficult people in Britain and Europe, and infusing moral strength into despairing statesmen. There was Roman strength in that frail figure, and deep sincerity— a strength based on faith and the inspiration of ideal resources. There was understanding, too, of Roman statesmanship, and of acceptance of non-Romans in recognition of progress. If he had lived, Smuts would probably have arrived at a graduated form of representation for non-whites.

Smuts admired Cicero the Roman farmer who defended the growing cultural tradition of his country against those whose enthusiasm for the overseas product made them look down on the native arts. He admired, too, the Roman gift for law and organisation, which was applied with greater skill than by Greek rulers. The Romans built up important and extensive codes of law, widely used to this day in International Law. He admired the early efforts to create a literature. He admired even more the Roman capacity for learning to grow beyond the fear-based attitude of self-centred nationalism. He admired the resourcefulness of the Roman in conducting war, if the motives justified it, though there were naturally times when national prejudice prevailed. He admired the Romans' understanding of non-Roman people. He realised that Greek culture was a priceless heritage that must be saved; so that when he saw the tomb of Archimedes fallen into neglect at Syracuse, he spent time and money to get it repaired. He wanted to use the resources of Rome to preserve Greek culture, as part of the bilingual Roman tradition, just as he wanted English culture in South Africa to be preserved side by side with Afrikaans, as part of the bilingual South African tradition; for both had an individual character that could contribute to the Whole.

An important aspect of Holism for Smuts was the realisation that narrow nationalism would only lead to impoverishment. Smuts saw beyond the immediate questions of his day, as Cicero did. Cicero faced the problems of maintaining the principles of democracy in abnormal times, and was accused of inconsistency. But he strove, like Smuts, in the direction of *humanitas*. Both fought passionately against the idea and practice of dictatorship. Both fought for a human peace based on the goodwill of nations. Both avoided sentimental abstract racial generalisations. The Romans used to send a commission to confer with the conquered people in their own country, and to ascertain what native institutions had been successful and could be continued. On that experience, and not on theoretical argument, the new law of the province was built up. That was what Smuts tried in the confused assembly of the United Nations, to base the new order on past experience. But, like Cicero, he had little success.

Cicero, after a life of practical politics, wrote in his book *On Duties*, a year before his death; 'To take away privileges from another, so that one person may profit by the loss of another, . . . strikes at the roots of human society and fellowship. . . . Nature prescribes that every human being should help every other human being, whoever he is, just because they are all fellow beings. Some think we should take account of compatriots but not foreigners; but this is to upset the whole basis of a community. . . . Nature has joined mankind together in one community'. One of the speakers in Cicero's *Republic* observes that, 'the whole universe is controlled by a single mind'.

Such holistic sentiments were very much in Smuts's line of thought, even if he modified individual opinions. As a student of Roman Law he would have endorsed another statement in the *Republic*: 'There will not be one law at Rome, one at Athens, or one now and one later; but all nations will be subject all the time to this one changeless and everlasting law, and one God will be shared by all of us, our Master and our Ruler—God who invented and instituted this law and arbitrates its operation' (transl. Michael Grant). Such has been the faith and ideal of enlightened people through the ages. But rulers exercising their free will have not, alas, acted in accordance with it, either in ancient or in modern times.

On April 22, 1919, Alice Clark, sister of Margaret Gillett, wrote to Oom Jannie: 'God has made us to live by mutual service and helpfulness, and the building, whether of national or personal life, on the basis of selfishness will come to nothing, because it has no bottom to it.' And later, 23 April, 1919: 'I find myself in a world where despair already seems to have settled on men's souls. Despair and a solemn belief in words and talk.' Such was the insight of Alice Clark. On 24 April, 1919, Smuts wrote to her that they (the victors) must make a tremendous appeal to the spirit of self-sacrifice, which alone would help them through the peace, as it had helped them through the war. Alice Clark (to Smuts, 25 April, 1919) referred to 'the small and trivial intellects which are so busy talking around you, and patching together treaties and ideas which have no roots in the divine, universal mind, which creates all things that exist'. These were anxious days for the peace of the world, and the mind was driven back on fundamental principles, beyond the selfishness of party-politicians. But Alice Clark also gave practical advice (26 April, 1919). 'Ask people for energy, determination, intelligence, co-operation, good sense, courage. And give the promise that when they have saved the world, they will have saved themselves too.'

Many practical things had to be done. The achievement of the Commonwealth of Nations, to supersede the old idea of Imperial Rule, was a triumph for Smuts and held great promise for the future, if only people would realise it. Many difficulties lay ahead; yet in spite of failure, the ideal remains. Smuts, in the despair and confusion that again marked the end of the Second World War, hoped that 'The Voices (of the spirit) will once more speak to us like long ago, and we shall once more be at rest'. (Letter to Margaret Gillett, Feb. 1945).

When Smuts was returning to South Africa on the Edinburgh Castle in July, 1919, he reflected ruefully that he had spent five years on recent war business, and eight including the period of the South African War; he added a prayer that this experience would not come again, that there would be a healing of the nations. Little did he realise that his bitterest war experience was still to come, that the nations were still far from healed (*Smuts Papers*, IV. p. 277).

His military activities have been fully recorded and are available for consultation. But they did not represent the interests he had at heart. When an American botanist consulted him on certain grasses, he gave her such detailed information that she asked him how he, a General, found time for such study; to which he replied: 'Madam, I am a General only in my spare time.' His main concern was always the peace of his nation or the nations of the world; the interest in Holism was an attempt to reconcile opposing forces, to help the process of evolution to a form of harmony, to find a Whole.

At the end of the First World War, when peace was being discussed, his letters to his Quaker friends reveal an anguish of spirit that is heart-rending. I believe his feelings were genuine, not verbal displays in a party-political game. He never forgot that he had been generously treated by Campbell-Bannerman after Vereeniging, and he wanted to show a similar spirit to his opponents in Europe. He decided not to sign the proposed peace-treaty, but mass pressure and consideration for Botha's position caused him to change his mind. He did so with deep misgiving, and after publishing a strong protest.

Smuts later recalled the famous prayer Botha wrote, as he listened to the vindictive utterances around him.

'In the Hall of Mirrors at Versailles on 28 June, 1919, the German representatives were called up to sign the Peace Treaty and to undergo the greatest humiliation to which it was possible to subject the haughty German Empire. He (Botha) first surveyed the whole scene and then bent over his agenda paper and wrote the following words on it, in his peculiar kind of Dutch-Afrikaans, at a time when linguistic forms were still in a stage of transition:

'God's judgement will be applied with justice to all peoples under the new sun, and we shall persevere in the prayer that they may be applied to mankind in charity and peace and a Christian spirit. To-day I think back to 31 May 1902.' (The Treaty of Vereeniging at the end of the South African War).

'Great words,' commented Smuts, 'coming from a

great heart, which had itself suffered much in the past, and could feel deep pity for the enemy in the hour of his downfall. That prayer of Louis Botha deserves to be written on the heart of the people of South Africa, ay, of the whole world, in the difficult period upon which we are now entering.'

From early days at Stellenbosch Smuts had the characteristic of looking beyond his immediate surroundings. As a student he was never tied down by the curriculum. Life to him was an expanding creative force, something more than the addition of parts, and not confined to the strait waistcoat of dogma. In his early essay *Homo sum* he asked whether impersonal law contained the highest truth; the answer was not law, but human personality. Personality retained its rights even when wrong decisions had been made. His thoughts on the peace terms proposed in 1919 are therefore instructive.

On May 2, 1919, he wrote to Alice Clark: 'I am much troubled over our peace terms. I consider them bad. And wrong. And they may not be accepted. The world may lapse into complete chaos.' 'I am getting more and more uneasy,' he said later, 'over the terms of peace . . . they will leave a trail of anarchy, ruin and bitterness in their wake for another generation.' To Alice Clark again on 7 May, 1919, he wrote: 'I am not enamoured of our so-called peace terms. Sometimes they appear to have been conceived more in the spirit of making war than of making peace. . . . Behind the pretty stage on which we pose and strut and play-act, looms the dark Figure which is quietly moving the pieces of world history. . . . But God is everywhere, according to your creed as well as mine, and maybe He is shaping a new world behind the polluted atmosphere and tenebrous mists of our poor

Conference.' 'My mind will go back to another May day in 1902, when peace terms were handed to the Boers, and in less than five years, those terms had been blown to smithereens by fate.' 'The Treaty impresses me with a sense of how much hate and fear blind people.'

Alice Clark wrote to him (18 May, 1919) 'At Vereeniging you laid down the weapons and continued the struggle in the field of diplomacy. This time the sword and gun were successful, but the wrestle with spiritual wickedness has been in the high places at Paris, and you appear to have lost once more. . . .' 'You have done your best to change and modify the report (of the peace terms), but your coadjutors are prejudiced and have refused to listen to you. . . . It is a very bad business.'

Smuts to Margaret Gillett: 'I understand the Prime Minister (Lloyd George) is very angry with me. Wilson is also failing me. He is not really a great man and Clemenceau has proved too strong both for him and our mercurial, tricky Prime Minister.' 'I have just written to Isie the conclusions to which I have come in regard to this Peace Treaty. It is so bad that I have decided not to sign unless important alterations are made in it.' To Alice Clark (23.5.1919) 'The Peace Conference has been a great failure. . . . The spirit has been very bad . . . I see dark days ahead.'

Smuts had no illusions about the guilt of the Germans and the fact that they must pay heavily for their aggression. But he did not want the contribution that a reformed Germany could make to Europe to be destroyed. He realised that the Quaker idealism of his friends could not always pass muster at the Conference table. But much of their insight and faith was justified in subsequent years. They were ahead of their time. He must later have thought back to what Margaret Gillett wrote (27.6.1919), referring to the manifesto that followed his decision to sign after all:

'If you had refused to sign, that would have made your statement in itself more possible. If you do sign, you must make your statement more forcible and convincing. There is some weakness inasmuch as you don't and perhaps can't give the true reason why you sign.' Smuts's people at Doornkloof, especially Isie, did not want him to sign either. Previously Alice Clark had written: '. . . the end is not yet.'

No, indeed. There was still the shattering onset of the Nazi attack to come. Could it have been modified or averted by a moderate peace treaty, such as Smuts desired? The moral issue was inescapable. For ten years I worked on *The Forum* and advocated *humanitas* and the civilized attitude in race relations. There was also our paper *Suid-Afrika*, trying to preach the same message in Afrikaans; it was unfortunately badly edited. The tide was against us. But the efforts were genuine, and in line with Smuts's thought and the values of his Quaker friends.

So once more Oom Jannie was involved in war. Not because he was fond of fighting, but because of his principles. Outwardly, there was the business of party-political plots and counter plots. Smuts foresaw many of the events in the war that came to pass, but the fundamental concern in his attitude was the moral issue. 'Shall we never learn the lesson?' he wrote at the beginning of the Second World War. The Paris Conference that followed it in 1946 raised hopes, but ended in the disappointment he anticipated. 'There is no solution through war. This war, whatever the ultimate issue, will be followed by another peace, which may be no peace; for after devastating conflict, there is no mood for a real and wise peace. . . . Meanwhile, civilization is falling back and the light of the Spirit is being dimmed . . . and so the caravan passes once more into the night. May God be with us and take the hands of His erring children.'

'For me, personally, there was no other way. I am a firm believer in the Commonwealth, not only for its own sake and for that of South Africa, but as the first tentative beginnings of great things for the future of the world. I was not going to desert or betray that great cause.' Again he achieved great things in international politics, as well as the conduct of the war, and he received enormous acclamation. Perhaps too much.

This was Smuts the Roman, with his sense of law and statesmanship, of constitutional development, of military affairs, of international co-operation, of human relationships, of ultimate moral values, of the way to enrich cultural life by fostering the second language, of balanced judgement in desperate circumstances. It was a task of many and various implications and countless pitfalls, incredibly wide in its implications, and one that unfortunately exposed him to criticisms from people who were not in a position to grasp the Whole.

CHAPTER V

SMUTS OF SOUTH AFRICA

At the bottom of Government Avenue in Cape Town schoolboys were playing marbles. General Smuts came out of Parliament House after weighty Parliamentary debates and saw them. He stopped and said: 'No, no, my boy, that is not the way to hold your marble when you want to shoot.' And he dropped on one knee and took the marble and demonstrated to the child the correct way of holding it.

That was typical of the lively, many-sided Oom Jannie. He comes from a debate on high politics, but finds time to encourage children playing marbles.

About this time he said to me, talking about J. H. Hofmeyr, 'He wants to be too much like Christ in the rough-and-tumble of party politics. Of course,' he added, 'I am rather like that myself.' He recognised the contrast between the low technique of party political argument and the ideals of government that were fundamental to himself and to J. H. Hofmeyr.

Once, in 1911, I was standing with Hoffie in the court of the old South African College, opposite the so-called Egyptian building. I asked him what he intended to do after his University career. He said: 'Politics.' I replied: 'You will find it a low-down game. It will break your heart.' It did. Time after time I went to see him during my association with *The Forum*, which he asked me to join as assistant editor; I could see the saddening look on his face become more and more pronounced. The conflict

40

between his ideals and the exigencies of party was wearing him down. He felt it as deeply as Smuts did. But the lively mind of Smuts could throw it off; the mind of Hofmeyr could not. Politics was his blind spot.

There were some things that Oom Jannie did not fully realise. One was the depth of feeling that the Afrikaner had for the Afrikaans language. There had been the avowed intention of Milner to root out Afrikaner language and sentiment. There had been a time when 'culture' in South Africa was English and nothing else. There had been the opposition of the Hollanders, who said 'Afrikaans has no grammar. We must promote a simplified Nederlands in the place of Afrikaans'. There had been Directors of Education who saw no point in encouraging Afrikaans. There had been the superior attitude of English people who sneered at the simple beginnings of Afrikaans literature.

The result was that when Afrikaans literature took shape, the feeling among Afrikaners for their language, which had steered a perilous course between Dutch opposition and English contempt, took on a disproportionate intensity. People talked later, when they looked back, about the Miracle of Afrikaans—its survival indeed was almost incredible. In 1903, when Chamberlain visited Pretoria, Smuts spoke in Afrikaans, using an interpreter. He wished to emphasise the need for considering the position of Afrikaans.

Yet Smuts, who had grown up in the earlier period, did not quite understand the depth of feeling that was present in the later development and the advisability of showing an active interest in the growing Afrikaans literature. He did not appreciate the fresh genius of C.

Louis Leipoldt, a member of his own party, and a candidate at one of his elections.

Then there was the question of the two languages in the schools. Dr. E. G. Malherbe and I persuaded him to put through Parliament the proposal that South Africa should return to Hertzog's idea of dual-medium instruction, that is, the use of the second language not merely as a subject learned from text-books, but as a medium for teaching various subjects, such as history, as in Paul Roos's school at Stellenbosch. He was successful in getting the motion passed. He knew that one only learns a language when one uses it for conveying or acquiring knowledge. But stupid people in the Department in the Transvaal misapplied this idea by forcing the time factor unreasonably, and so a good principle was spoiled and withdrawn by the very Government which had proposed it. The English-speaking population was partly responsible for this. The result is that both the Afrikaans and English-speaking sections now think in terms of separate schools; as the Administrator of the Cape reported a while ago, large areas in the Republic are becoming unilingual, and separation is causing ignorance and estrangement.

Two conversations I shall never forget. The one took place at St. John's College, Johannesburg. We were discussing the possibility of dual-medium education with the idea that both language-groups should be represented in the school. I am sure most of the staff were in favour of this. But one of the Governing Body said to me: 'We don't want Afrikaners in the school, we don't want Jews, we want Anglicans.' In actual fact there were Afrikaners and there were Jews. But many people supported this

42

opinion, and it was repeated in private, even if not voiced in public.

The other conversation was with Paul Roos, the redoubtable first Springbok captain, headmaster in Stellenbosch. Looking back on his honest efforts to establish a dual-medium system, one which produced perfectly bilingual citizens like Professor Arthur Bleksley, he said sadly: 'There was no response. Not a single English-medium school followed our example.' The result was that in the end the Afrikaans teachers' associations plumped heavily for separate-medium schools, with Afrikaans as the only medium of instruction. That is the position to-day.

But when I was on the staff of Stellenbosch University a few years ago, I found a number of students from 'Bishops', the Rondebosch Diocesan College, and other English-medium schools, who voluntarily came to an Afrikaans-medium University because they felt that their South African education was incomplete, their training being in Afrikaans merely as a subject, with no practice in its use for acquiring information, and for expressing themselves. They were ahead of the formal regulation. They felt they had not achieved a Whole in citizenship.

Contact between young children of the two groups is very important. If the dual-medium is despaired of, there could at least be the parallel-medium system under which each group would use its own medium, but would have the advantage of associating with the other group and learning its language by doing things together. Here, too, a Whole could be created.

There was a niece of mine, aged six, who came to stay with my parents in Stellenbosch. Her people were working as missionaries in Central Africa and her home language was English. We thought we had better continue her tradition by speaking English to her. But next door were Afrikaans-speaking children of her own age who became friendly. Within three months this niece was fully bilingual. She learned to speak to the children next door, with whom she played in spontaneous association. Thus she became proficient in the second language much more quickly than she would have done through lessons in school, learning Afrikaans as a subject. The natural urge is for children to mix and talk spontaneously, even at the stage when their education is supposed to be based on the mother tongue. The children find Holism natural; it is the grown-ups who put up barriers. If only we could create a natural atmosphere and leave the children to it! To them differences of race and tongue are not barriers. Gilbert Murray, describing the world of Ovid's *Metamorphoses*, writes of 'a world of wonderful children where nobody is really cross or wicked except the grown-ups.' We have a grave responsibility to our young people. We should consider their growing souls, not the part their elders want them to play in the world of state or church.

Grown-ups often forget that their own thoughts and acts provide barriers for children. Thoughts are things. If you want children to be enthusiastic you must reveal enthusiasm yourself. Horace realised that. Abstract teaching, however efficient, will not prove effective. If you think in terms of separateness, political or religious, that thought will pass to the children and erect a barrier. The quality of our thinking is therefore of great importance. The thought in the home must be constructive and creative, to produce a like attitude in the children; not Christian-National in the narrow sense of party-

politics, but Christian-South African in the cause of
South Africa as a whole. South Africa first is what Smuts
felt, but not South Africa alone. The Afrikaner tradition
unimpaired, but fruitfully co-operating with the English
and European tradition, fertilising and being fertilised,
providing the full enrichment of which our various
cultural contacts are capable, and not excluding the non-
whites. That is a Whole, difficult indeed of attainment,
but surely worth striving for; a task demanding endless
patience and goodwill, endless perseverance and constructive effort, deep wisdom, but leading to the fulness
of life that Oom Jannie envisaged in his inner being.

In the tenth chapter of the Acts of the Apostles, there
is the story[1] of the Roman centurion Cornelius, 'a just
man and one that feareth God' (let us note that he is not
just a Pagan, to be separated and pushed aside; he is
capable of fearing God, the universal God). He is also 'of
good report among all the nation of the Jews'. He
receives a warning from God 'by an holy angel'. Again,
the messenger of God does not exclude Cornelius as a
Roman, but tells him to send for Peter and hear his words,
thereby showing that God will communicate with one
who is outside the Christian faith. Cornelius was so
impressed that he fell down and worshipped Peter, who
raised him up and said to the company: 'Ye know how
that it is an unlawful thing for a man that is a Jew to
keep company or come unto one of another nation;
but God (i.e. the universal God who transcends racial
barriers) hath shewed me that I should not call any man
common or unclean.' Peter goes on to say: 'Of a truth I
perceive that God is no respecter of persons', (He has no
favourites), 'but in every nation he that feareth him

[1] Used by Rev. Beyers Naude, 31.8.68, before the Christian Institute.

45

and worketh righteousness, is accepted with him . . . and we are witnesses of all things which he did both in the land of the Jews and in Jerusalem, (He) whom they slew and hanged on a tree; Him God raised up the third day and shewed him openly . . . .' The orthodox Jews were amazed—'they of the circumcision which believed were astonished . . . because that on the Gentiles also was poured out the gift of the Holy Ghost (the spirit of God)'. Peter then commanded that Cornelius and his friends should be baptised.

Here, then, we have a number of orthodox religious people who believed in separateness and considered themselves the Chosen Race; and we see the apostle of Christ, who is converted from the traditional belief in separateness and breaks down the old barriers to the astonishment of his fellow-Jews, proclaim the message of God to extend beyond the race concept of the religious, so as to include Romans like Cornelius. The intention of God is shown to be Whole-making; the line of division is not race but spirit and receptiveness.

Have we not here a parable for our time? We have heard a great deal lately about the word 'ecumenical'. It is from the Greek *oikoumenē* (with *gē* understood), the inhabited world, including all the people of the globe. There have been several movements in this direction, and many of the younger generation are thinking in these terms; but the much advertised Ecumenical Synod held in August, 1968, at Lunteren in Holland, was not ecumenical in the widest sense; it represented only Calvinists from different parts of the world. Even so, a resolution was passed that all church services should be held before unsegregated congregations, that is to say, that non-whites should worship side by side in the same church

46

with whites, and that Holy Communion should be admin-istered on these lines. This challenge is being taken up by members of the Nederduits Gereformeerde Kerk of South Africa. The movement is further evidence of a tendency to bridge gaps between parts and form a Whole. We need to remind ourselves that the Greek *holos*, the English *whole* and the Afrikaans *heel* are all related to *hale* in English, and *heil* in Afrikaans, and so link up with *holy* in English and *heilig* in Afrikaans. In each language the idea contained is that of a healthy Whole. No one is complete in development until he has formed a *Whole* in body and spirit, a Whole on earth, and a Whole between heaven and earth. 'On earth the broken arcs, in heaven a perfect round', as Browning wrote. The prayer of Christ for his followers is still far from realisation, 'that they all may be one', *ut omnes unum sint*; again the idea of the perfect *Whole*.

We start in the physical world with the obvious fact that Nature is a healer, a Whole-maker. The plant that loses a twig while it is still in good condition repairs the loss without help from outside; so with the animal that has suffered a wound that is not fatal; and so, too, the human being. There is a Whole-making process in Nature that operates under normal circumstances inde-pendently of our help. Hippocrates, the Father of Medicine, said Nature was the Healer, and more import-ant than the doctors. This is a fundamental point in the philosophy of Holism. In the biological world the evidence is there for all to see. In the world of physics it is not so easy; but the eminent scientists should have the final word with the reader.

Professor J. S. Haldane, father of the famous J. B. S. Haldane, writing in the *Hibbert Journal* of April, 1923, rejected altogether the mechanistic explanation of life, chiefly on the ground that the upholders of the theory had failed to look at life as a whole, and had based their conclusions on fragments and abstractions. They had disregarded Holism. 'The fundamental conceptions of physical science,' he says, 'represent only working hypotheses, corresponding under great limitations to partial aspects of experience. Extraordinarily useful as these working hypotheses are, in the absence of more detailed knowledge, they do not represent reality. This appears at once when we consider our experience as a whole. It is only when we neglect this consideration that we seem driven to a materialistic creed.' Elsewhere he maintains that 'the only real world is the spiritual world, the only real values, spiritual values'; these imply stages in the development of culture.

Max Planck, the mathematical physicist, and Rector Magnificus of the University of Berlin where we studied, wrote in *Nature*, 18th April, 1931; 'It is the concept of wholeness that must be introduced into the field of physics, as well as into the field of biology, in order to enable us to understand and formulate the laws of nature'. Schrödinger and Heisenberg expanded this idea.

Smuts held (Cf. *Smuts Papers* I. 60) that behind life there is something we cannot formulate, a mysterious force that is its source. In short, there remains the mystery of the transcendental ego. Everything is in the process of change. The times in which we live, Smuts said at the end of the First World War, do not really permit of rigid opinions or of any dogmatic outlook on life. (J. C. Smuts, Life of his father, p. 441).

Smuts preferred to speak of processes, tendencies and forces in Nature that may be Whole-making. The completion of a process may give us a new Whole, as a plant restores a broken member without external aid. The new Whole may be, generally is, only temporary, but even so it represents a stage achieved which is better than a mere fragment.

CHAPTER VI

EXAMPLES OF HOLISM IN THE CLASSICS AND THE BIBLE

A work of art is an organic whole in which the total conception is quite different from the aggregate of its separate parts. As Aristotle said, a work of art is like a living animal, not like a machine. It shows growth and development. You cannot remove one part and fit in another from some other source. Organic unity makes it necessary to understand any art form as a whole.

For example, Homer's *Iliad* starts with the wrath of Achilles, arising from the arbitrary insult of Agamemnon, who deprived him of Briseis, the girl who had been allotted to him legitimately. This causes strife among the Greeks and the withdrawal of Achilles, without whom the Greeks are lost. Attempts at reconciliation fail. Finally Patroclus, the bosom friend of Achilles, goes forth to battle wearing the armour of Achilles, and he prevails because the Trojans think Achilles has returned. But Hector kills Patroclus, and Achilles loses the friend who means more to him than Briseis or anyone else; and so he is roused to return to the war and kills Hector. And now Achilles begins to realise the folly of all anger and violence, first the loss of Briseis through the action of Agamemnon, and then the loss of Patroclus through his own action. Is it not time to put wrath aside in his deep sorrow for Patroclus? The first word in the first book of the poem is *Mēnin*, from *Mēnis*, wrath; the final scene in the last book, the twenty-fourth, where Achilles goes to Priam to

restore the body of his son Hector is an act of concilia-
tion, a rejection of *Mēnis*, especially significant as religious
importance was attached to burial. The organic unity in
the theme of Wrath is shown in the victory, or the
attempted victory over Wrath in the last Book. In spite
of all the discrepancies and disputes, organic growth and
balanced treatment indicate the artistic purpose of the
poet, whom we traditionally call Homer.

But what is the usual procedure in reading the text?
There is not time in the ordinary curriculum to read more
than a few books; and student attention has to be concentrated almost exclusively on the grammar and linguistic
meaning. In talking to students, I have found that they
are usually ignorant of the course and construction of the
story. The lecturer's analysis of the text has left them no
time for literary investigation. To remedy this, I introduced a system by which they read two or three books in
the original, and completed the reading in translation. In
this way, we sought to achieve a whole and to see the plan
the author had in mind. Since then I have found that
overseas universities, including Oxford, have adopted a
similar scheme.

The same method is applied to the Roman epic,
Vergil's *Aeneid*. Very few, even of Honours students,
read the twelve books as a whole and try to see the structure and the organic development. The main theme of
this epic is announced at the beginning (I. 32); the birth
of the Roman nation and the travail that attended its
growth. The war that arose from the clash of races and
the struggle for supremacy is described as *dirum*, accursed,
by Vergil. The springboard of his thought is the founding
of a new home for the exiles from Troy, the city that will
serve, in time, to build a new Whole. The crux is the

existence of different racial elements, and the task to weld them into a co-operative state, creating unity out of diversity. Among the different Italian tribes, speaking different languages there were the Etruscans, probably of Asiatic origin; there were also the Celts with their passionate natures; there were the Greeks who were to supply the culture and second language in an ultimately bi-lingual Rome. Out of this diversity was to come a Roman civilisation that provided the cultural basis of later Western Europe. The Etruscans actually conquered Rome in the beginning, and their kings were established there. They made their contribution to Roman art and to the organisation of the state; so that in the Augustan Age Horace recorded that Maecenas was proud of his Tuscan descent. Celtic elements are found in Catullus and Vergil, and the liveliness of Roman comedy owed a great deal to the Italian (as distinct from the Roman) character. Roman law and oratory show the influence of the ruling city, and reflect 'the immense majesty of the Roman Peace', as Pliny the Elder called it. Empires are not popular to-day, but Roman rule preserved order and built up the tremendous contribution of Roman Law, in its successive codes. This Whole is still of vital importance to-day.

The first real friend whom Aeneas finds in the *Aeneid* is not Dido, not even an Italian, though Latinus, the king, had been friendly at first; he was a Greek from Arcadia, Evander. Vergil thus indicates the importance of future Greek-Roman co-operation. The two languages and the two cultures are to form a Whole. Roman literature is to maintain its individuality, but to be enriched by the Greek genius. In South Africa, Smuts saw the Afrikaner element maintaining its individuality, but enriched by the English-European tradition.

Latin is a dead language only in the sense that no nation actually speaks it to-day. Sir D'Arcy Thompson, the scientist who was also a classical scholar, pointed out that for those who can appreciate it, Latin literature can be as lively as any modern literature. 'Is that old Italian speech dead and gone,' he asks, 'that murmurs in Lucretius a ceaseless solemn monotone of sea-shell sound; that in Vergil flows, like the Eridanus, calmly and majestically through rich lowlands, fringed with tall poplars and rimmed with grassy banks; that quivers to wild strains of passion in Catullus; that wimples like a beck in Ovid; that coos in Tibullus like the turtle; that sparkles in Horace like a well-cut diamond?' (*Science and the Classics*; Proceedings of the Classical Association, 1929). The beauty is often destroyed by analysis and exaggerated attention to portions devoid of their context. Let us read the sentences as wholes, in their Latin order, and get the feeling of them as well as the meaning. This is one form of Holism. But there is another: to connect the written with the spoken form. The sound of Latin is of great importance for its understanding and appreciation. In our reading we must not be content with snippets. We must study the work as a whole, from the human side. Caesar is not merely a book, he is also a man. Dr. L. P. Jacks, long the editor of the *Hibbert Journal*, wrote; 'The modern man is at his best when he is dealing with analysis—his recent education has all tended in that direction. But he is something of a blockhead when it comes to synthesis. For breaking a thing up into parts and studying each part in separation, there never has been anybody to compare with the modern man.' (L. P. Jacks: *The Education of the Whole Man*, 1931). But to get him to think synoptically is another matter. 'Wholeness' seems to baffle him.

53

The completion that art gives to nature, according to Aristotle, raises various questions. At first sight it would seem that Wholeness is the last thing we should find in modern art. But there is the wholeness of the artist's dedication to his art, and his quest to 'complete what nature is unable to elaborate'. Here he is held by the conventions of his age, and we should try to understand what his intentions are, in terms of the modern fashion.

Greek art of the sixth and fifth centuries B.C. did try to see life steadily and see it whole. Roman sculpture excelled in portrait studies, and probably owed its realism to the Etruscans. The Roman paintings of Pompeii show developments of perspective, and sometimes the representation of plants, flowers and animals, which we do not find in Greek art.

Smuts says more than once of the world of science 'The whole is more than the sum of its parts'; and this is true also of the world of literature. Aristotle said there must be a necessary or probable connection between the parts of a tragedy, a growth and a sense of inevitability.

Series iuncturaque pollent, Horace told us; 'it is sequence and connection that count'. We must find the right links between things; and this is fundamental to Smuts's philosophy. There are people who spend their time looking for the things that separate, and try to make these into principles of life. That is the impoverishing type of mind. Wise teachers try to make things interesting by showing how they are related. What we take for dulness in children is often a failure on our parts to stimulate interest. We over-simplify. We should set the big things before the minds of children—a play of Shakespeare, for example. They may fail to understand much of it, but contacts are made, and echoes remain in the mind to bear fruit later. More good literature, explained to illustrate the purpose of the whole, should be read aloud. But to do this the teacher must himself be a lover of the beautiful, an enthusiast for the whole. Only so can he make his pupils keen.

St. Augustine said: *Ex amante alio accenditur alius*, 'one loving spirit sets another on fire'.

Texts quoted in separation can be used for almost any purpose. How few teachers encourage their pupils to read the Bible books, as wholes! How few adults have made the experiment of reading, for example, the Gospel of St. Mark as a whole! The Bible is not a single book, but a library written at different times, and containing widely differing ethical standards. The books should be read as Wholes and related to the time of their composition. The enormous influence of our Bible can only be understood if we read it in a spirit of universal understanding, and not as the property of particular sects. Literalism is always misleading, and the Bible was never meant to be read like that. Its meaning in history is of tremendous importance, and Smuts realised this. Among the bitterest opponents of Jesus (and let us remember that the actual recording of His mission occurred a generation after His death) were the people who were supposed to be religious leaders, but who often failed to appreciate the inspirational nature of the Message.

Ut omnes unum sint, 'that they all may be one', was the prayer of Jesus for His followers. I have gone through the Latin records of the Church Councils, beginning in the 4th Century A.D., which aimed at formulating an orthodox belief. What a spectacle! What bitter attacks of members on one another, because of differences of opinion natural to men with different backgrounds.

These differences called for tolerance and understanding; they did not affect fundamental principles. There followed the subsequent quarrels inside the Church, the persecutions, the burnings, the destruction.

There is, we have seen, an attempt to-day to get back to the universal spirit of Christianity. Each Church is to retain its dogma and ritual, and pray that the other Churches will regard these with tolerance.

J. H. Hofmeyr used to say: 'Christianity is a universal religion, if you understand its essential nature'; and Smuts realised the truth of this, particularly when he came to evaluate personality. 'To the evolution of the modern idea of Personality, Christianity made the most notable contribution in investing the human being as such with a character of sacredness, of spiritual dignity and importance, which implied a far-reaching revolution in ethical ideas. The Roman legal concept thus became blended with the moral sacredness and inalienable rights of human beings as children of God. . . . It has been my endeavour . . . to trace the concept of Personality to its real relationships . . . to show it . . . as a real factor which forms the culminating phase in the synthetic creative Evolution of the Universe. . . . The Christian traced Personality to the fatherhood of God, which conferred it on all human beings as a sacred birthright. Here Personality becomes the last item in the holistic series . . .' (*Holism and Evolution*, 292).

In a letter to Isie (12.5.1902), Smuts wrote: 'During these last twelve months I have read much of the writings of the citizens of this larger country, whose foundations and codes are far beyond the imperialism of this twentieth century—citizens like Isaiah, Thomas à Kempis, Augustine, Kant, Goethe and others belonging to all ages, but

56

all of the kingdom of which Jesus Christ is the first citizen.'

On 16.5.1919, to Alice Clark: 'Yes, that was a great experience on the hills. I always hold that you come most into direct contact with the Divine in moments of great isolation and loneliness. Not for nothing did the great Inspirer go into the desert or in the lonely hills for inspiration. The crowd is great; where two or three are gathered together in the great name is a holy place. But holier still is that place where the lonely, wounded human spirit clasps the Divine Spirit, and Holism is consummated.'

That was Oom Jannie's experience of Whole-making in its highest form. Alice Clark shared that experience with him. 'Our whole being,' she wrote to him (30.4.1919) 'is continually transformed and renewed according to the divine purpose.' She speaks of 'the harmony of mutual service', and adds 'you see this is holism'. She tells him of 'the application on the practical side of this attitude, to the divine whole, which is energy and creative power'. And on 21.6.1919 he wrote to Margaret Gillett: 'The kingdom of God is within you', not in outward manifestations.

Many of Smuts's thoughts were never published, and most remained incomplete. This I realised in conversations I had with him. To Leif Egeland he said in 1949 that there were three things he still wanted to do (1) to revise his book on Holism, (2) to write a biography of Paul Kruger and (3) to compile a survey of the flora of Africa. None of these aims did he live to achieve.

Among the people who understood him best was Professor J. I. Marais of the Theological Seminary at Stellenbosch, a wise and good man, capable of appreciat-

ing the qualities of Jan Smuts. There was also Monsignor
F. C. Kolbe, son of a Protestant minister who became a
Catholic. Hancock pays a just tribute to these two men.

Smuts sent his book on Holism to Kolbe, who warned
Oom Jannie of the opposition it would arouse. On a
first reading he said to a friend: 'This is a *deeply* religious
book'. He could see the motive power behind the idea of
Holism; but there were many contradictions and con-
troversial assertions. Kolbe noted the resemblance
between the *Telos*, the End, of Aristotle, and Smuts's
Whole; also the indebtedness to Thomas Aquinas. He
directed Smuts to the first chapter of St. John's Gospel,
and its doctrine of the *Logos*. Smuts once told Gilbert
Murray that Holism represented his faith, and that
without this faith he could not have got through life
(*Hancock* I. 197).

Some of the criticism evoked by Holism seems
incredible and may have been deliberately perverse. To
speak of *tribalism* and *a devilish totalitarian invention* in
connection with Smuts, after his work for the League of
Nations is the height of absurdity. Smuts spent four
strenuous years fighting totalitarianism and the glorification of the State in Nazi philosophy.

There was, however, an important review of Smuts's
Holism by the late Professor F. Clarke, formerly Professor
of Education in the University of Cape Town; it appeared
in *The Cape Times* of 13.6.1927, to which Dr. E. G.
Malherbe drew my attention. Clarke considered the
application of Holism to education and drew attention to
the shattering of the old faiths. The serene self-assurance
of the Victorians, he says, has passed away. The robust
faith that Smuts displays is therefore encouraging. 'For
it is faith above all things that education and educators

58

need to-day. . . . Behind our striving towards betterment are, in the last resort, the entire weight and momentum, and the inmost nature and trend, of the Universe'. We are all embarked on the same kind of adventure, the discovery of truth; the universe is alive and active, and above all a learning universe, experimental and creative. Holism can be applied to education, first of all in the realm of child psychology, said Clarke. Modern child psychology is learning to think holistically, and we 'can be grateful to General Smuts for his philosophy of a universe which is itself one vast pupil. Being a great pupil, it is also a great schoolmaster, and the real business of the educator is to discover the methods of its teaching, and then humbly set himself in line with them.'

Chapter VII

THE UNDEVELOPED PEOPLE

One of our prominent scientists, Fred Hoyle, in *Man and Materialism*, said: 'The coloured peoples are accepting wholeheartedly the white man's technology, but they are not accepting in any real degree the rest of the white man's culture. Indeed, the white man is often actively despised for the rest of his culture' (p. 114).

Lady Moore, writing in April 1947, said: 'I see no possibility of compromise on the colour question; either the white race fights for its supremacy, confident of its superiority, or we admit that all men are alike under God, and that Christianity and the other codes of ethics in which we believe make no distinction between a white skin and a brown. So why should we? The trouble is that the subject is one which it is difficult to be logical about, because of the underlying fear, repulsion or whatever it is that the white man feels for the black, and which to you in South Africa, with generations of colour-strife in your blood, is an essential element in your characters, of which you are almost unaware. English people with their copy-book maxims and their smug humanitarian theories, cannot understand the instinct inherited from forebears, who have had to fight black races for their existence.'

She referred to Smuts's dilemma (which H. A. Fagan, Minister of Native Affairs in Hertzog's Cabinet, understood only too well). She continued: 'Not only are there the two sides to your nature you speak of—the humanitarian and the South African—but there are the people by whose vote you rule South Africa, many among them hopelessly bigoted and deaf to reason on the colour subject, but liable to turn extremist and ruin the future of South Africa, should they lose their faith in you and your policies.'

Lady Moore ably analysed the race problem, but she did not suggest anything constructive. Henry Fagan did. He saw the practical difficulties confronting Smuts, his dependence on future opinion and the possibility of his not being re-elected. Yet Smuts approved of Fagan's attitude. He accepted the principles of the Fagan Report.

It was characteristic of Smuts that he refused to take a rigid line. He saw that there must be growth in ideas of government in proportion as the people governed were capable of development. But he believed in South Africa as a whole; white and black must work together. 'We need them,' he often said, 'and they need us.' He felt concerned about the uprooted urban native, and wanted to help those who were in a de-tribalised state, without any organised social expression.

Fagan's commission made its report in 1948. It proposed that black South Africans, including the women and children, should be regarded as a permanent part of the urban population, and consequently would have to be taken into account by future legislators. It opposed territorial separation of the races as impracticable and based on wishful thinking. It rejected the practice of migratory labour. Some control over the movement of non-whites to the cities was condoned, but the idea that they could only come into the towns to serve the interests of the whites, and that this should be a rule, was not accepted.

In 1920 certain principles had been approved that seemed to be a step in progressive thinking. The Native Affairs Bill was called 'wise and generous', at this date, by so radical a paper as the *New Statesman*, and Smuts's speech on the subject was generally applauded. General Hertzog, while supporting the Bill, called for the abolition of the Cape franchise for the Coloured people. These points are mentioned, not as arguments in party-politics, but to show that in judging Smuts's action we must take into account the background of the time in which he lived, the swift changes in political opinion, and the exigencies of practical politics. He pleaded for happier relationships between black and white, and the regulations planned were to come one step at a time. He wanted conferences and consultations on the breaking up of tribal and family life, and the rapid entry of non-whites into industry. He stressed (perhaps insufficiently) the need to consider the urban conditions of African life; for the haphazard attitude of municipalities had led to disease and chaos. There was widespread ignorance of African ideas and customs, which produced misunderstanding and enmity. He said the Natives should be able to advise in the regulation of their own affairs. They should run their own shops and brew their own beer. These were opinions opposed to the popular ideas of the country.

In his Christmas message, 1923, Smuts said: 'White and Black both have a proper place in South Africa. Both have their human rights, and let us in fair and humble spirit approach the difficulties which arise out of them, and labour to make this land a home in which both races can live together in peace and friendship, and work out their salvation in fairness and justice.'

The Fagan Commission did not recommend total

abolition of the pass-laws, but it did propose that they should be modified and relaxed. It also proposed that there should be an organisation-of-labour bureau which would help to get labourers into employments that were suitable for them. The report was generally in the spirit of Smuts's philosophy. South African society was moving towards some show of dynamic development. There must be room not only for growth and experiment, but for the various groups to live together and help one another.

Smuts often found it difficult to square his principles with what was possible in the technique of interested politics. But his humane sense of values usually shone through and saved the situation.

A good example is the case of the Rain Queen, Modjadji, of which Hancock gives an interesting account. Smuts's daughter Cato (accent on the second syllable!), while travelling with her friend Eileen Jensen (later the wife of Jack Krige, Smuts's nephew), had a motor accident near the village of the Rain Queen, who received them with great friendliness. Smuts wrote to thank her personally and Isie sent a parcel of gifts. Eileen Jensen described a visit which Smuts paid later to the Rain Queen and noted that he 'never in the whole course of her close acquaintanceship with him treated the African as a child or an inferior'.

'Oom Jan,' she wrote in a letter (see *Hancock* II. 474) 'seemed instinctively to have the right touch. He was not put out by the fact that he was unacquainted with tribal procedure and Lovedu court etiquette. He behaved towards the queen in much the same way, and accorded her as much dignity, as I imagine he might have in the case of any diplomatic dignitary in Europe. He stood up when she came in, went up to her and shook hands, exchanged greetings and during the course of conversation referred to her kindness to Cato in the past. Jack and I discussed the scene later, and agreed that no advice which we as anthropologists could have given him, had we been asked, would have achieved what Oom Jan did by his natural, cordial manner. Oom Jan made a tremendous impression on the Lovedu court.'

This was typical. Qualities of character were often more effective as a bridge between people than correct formal procedures, and were longer remembered. They illustrated what Smuts meant when he said that there had been too much theorising about race relations. He believed in recognising the facts of unequal development.

The general public in South Africa, at any rate in the country districts, persists in thinking of colour as a line of demarcation; and this, as Lady Moore realised, is based on historical tradition. The book entitled *Culture* by F. R. Cowell (Thames and Hudson, 1959) suggests that the standard of culture attained by a particular group may be a more rational line of division.

What do we mean by culture?

'Culture,' says Cowell (p. 105), 'is that which being transmitted orally by tradition and objectively through writing and other means of expression, enhances the quality of life with meaning and value by making possible the formulation, progressive realization, appreciation and the achievement of truth, beauty and moral worth.'

Now culture is seen in varying degrees, and it is important to remember this when we refer to a standard of demarcation. There can be no formula, particularly when it comes to race. I have had a non-white student in my class at the University of Cape Town who earned the highest distinction in the highest Latin Course, and thoroughly deserved it. Similarly, I had an Indian student at the University of the Witwatersrand who earned a good First Class in Latin in the highest course. Both of them were men, not only of learning, but of culture. I knew an Indian at Oxford, afterwards a Cabinet Minister in India, who was not only a Christian of high quality, but the most learned and cultured of all the students I knew at the University. Race was certainly not a dividing line in those cases. In fact, as Professor B. B. Keet, late of the Theological College at Stellenbosch, once said, the only true dividing line is the ethical one, which accords with the idea of culture, as set forth by Cowell.

For the Coloured people Smuts felt deeply, but exigencies of party politics in later developments overshadowed his personal sympathies. In 1937 he supported J. H. Hofmeyr in obtaining benefits for all children, irrespective of race. He objected to the 'civilised labour policy', when it was interpreted as meaning white labour only. General Hertzog, the real founder of the Nationalist Party, was inclined to group the Coloureds with the Whites.

As a South African who thought of South Africa as a whole, Smuts saw the merits as well as the failings of the Coloured people. He realised their artistic possibilities, and admired the operatic performances of the Eoan Group. The Coloureds were born actors, he thought, and their work might enhance the status of South Africa in overseas opinion. In origin, they were closer to the Whites than the Africans, and therefore more easily understood. Their natural language was Afrikaans, and it would be a pity if, by insistence on colour alone, they were to be estranged by the Afrikaner. Smuts spoke highly of the Coloureds' services in the army. When treated with fairness, they responded with enthusiasm, as a general rule. He was against the formula of classifying them as inferiors; for he knew that they were at different levels of development; he appreciated progress and wished to help those who had made progress. He made special mention of them in 1947, during the royal visit to South Africa, when a welcome was accorded to the King, Queen and Princesses by the non-Whites. 'It is a good and sound people. . . . Our Coloured people were specially pleased with the attention shown to them. . . . This is just the sort of thing which Kings and Queens can do and which gives them a blessed and fruitful function in our human society. . . . Nowhere is it more wanted than in a land of races and colours, and nowhere can it render a greater service. Politics runs too high with us, and as the King is above all politics he becomes the reconciler and peace-maker.' (To Margaret Gillett, quoted *Hancock* II. 495).

Should we not avoid group-generalisation and think rather in terms of persons? 'Die diep vloek van 'n donker huid', the deep curse of a skin that's dark—that is the bitter cry of a Coloured poet, a man of sensitive and cultured feelings, who wrote in Afrikaans because that was natural to him. He was granted recognition as a poet by the Suid-Afrikaanse Akademie; but at a separate ceremony. He felt he was not one of the recognised community of Afrikaans poets. That estranged him—and no wonder. Colour counted more than culture; and there are others like him. That comes of recognising Colour as the dividing line between groups.

I should like to propose that every white South African should make it his duty to select a person of a different race, of suitable character and culture, and make a friend of him. There need be no exaggerated intimacy, but a sharing of interests and a desire to understand and discuss. I have had experience of this kind. First of all at the University of Cape Town with the Coloured student who won the medal in the third Latin Course; then with several others; there was friendship and helpfulness on both sides. Difference of colour interposed no barrier, because there was a linking of qualities of character and mutual understanding of problems. Interest attracts interest. If there had been to start with a rigid attitude of prejudice or repulsion on either side, sympathetic co-operation would not have been possible. Sometimes there is an initial hostility based on misunderstanding; but this can be overcome. Such was the beginning of my experience at Fort Hare. There was no friendly contact; just a blank wall. But this was overcome when I discovered that a member of the Latin class badly wanted a New Testament in Latin. I sent for a copy and presented it to him. This produced a transformation, not only because it was a gift, but because human interest had been shown in his progress. His attitude became friendly; he devoted himself to his studies; he became co-operative and the atmosphere was cleared.

In the senior class there was another Bantu student who was suspicious and tried to make trouble. If the attitude of cold authority had been taken up and a rigid reliance on disciplinary rules had been pursued, the situation would have remained dead and unfruitful, and the quality of the work unimproved. But by showing understanding and sympathy with difficulties, it was possible to create an atmosphere of co-operation which ripened into friendship, so that after I had left Fort Hare, this student began to write to me and discuss several problems. And he still does so, though our academic contact has long since come to an end.

Human friendship goes on in spite of differences of circumstance, and the dogmatic pronouncements by theorists about the gulf between one race and another. We found that we both welcomed the bridging of the gap. 'Die diep vloek van 'n donker huid'; what bitter feeling lies behind those words! What suffering and frustration!

The children of Ham, he said when he consulted me. Yes, in the Bible, Ham the son of Noah is cursed by his father, because when the father got drunk and took off his clothes, Ham, in contrast to his brothers Shem and Japhet, looked on his nakedness instead of bringing something to cover him (Genesis, Ch. 9). Was it true, my student asked, that the Coloured people were the descendants of Ham, and therefore not white? In the Psalms the Egyptians are referred to (it is thought) as the descendants of Ham (Ps. 25: 23, 27). The ancient Egyptian form was KEM, probably pronounced CHEM, which in the Dutch Bible is CHAM, and in Afrikaans GAM. The meaning is given as 'black' or 'sun-burnt', referring to the inhabitants. But some scholars interpret the word as referring to the black alluvial soil resulting from the overflow of the river. The inhabitants of Egypt can hardly be described as 'black' in appearance, and the connection between Egyptians and our Coloured people seems extremely tenuous. The name Egyptian seems to link up with the Greek *Aithops*, from *aitho*, to burn; hence sun-burnt. But the curse of Noah, 'Cursed be Canaan (the father of Ham), a servant of servants shall he be to his brethren' (Genesis 9:25), can only by a most unlikely stretch of imagination be connected with our people. General Smuts agreed with me—at least, so I gathered from the talks I had with him on the inhabitants of our country.

Discussions of this sort were possible without touching on political questions. Now this individual quest for friendship may be a slow process, but if everybody tried, there could be a considerable result. If you have found an individual whose friendship has lasted and stood the test of years, you have something constructive to build on for the future.

Smuts wrote to J. X. Merriman in 1906 (see *Smuts Papers* II. p. 242): 'It ought to be the policy of all parties to do justice to the natives and to take all wise and prudent measures for their civilization and improvement. Perhaps at bottom I do not believe in politics at all as a means for the attainment of the highest ends.'

The non-White question in South Africa never ceased to worry Smuts, especially when criticism outside South Africa concentrated more and more upon it. This is what Oom Jannie said: 'I personally am not against the native, I am against the policy of aggression. I would help the native in every legitimate way, in accordance with his present requirement. But I cannot forget that civilization has been built up in this country by the white race, and that we are the guardians of liberty, justice and all the elements of progress in South Africa. . . .

'We started as a small white colony in a black continent. In the Union the vast majority of our citizens are black, probably the majority of them are in a semi-barbarous state still, and we have never in our laws recognised any system of equality. It is the bedrock of our constitution. . . . That is the fundamental position from which we start.'

To many these sentiments may seem out-dated; but we should remember the circumstances of the time in which they were uttered.

I recently found in London a collection in progress for a Bantu student who wanted to study medicine in South Africa. It was argued that he had no place at home where he could pursue this study. But in fact there is an admirable medical school for Bantu students in Natal, Wentworth; it is also possible for them to get training at the Witwatersrant University, Johannesburg, as well as at the University of Cape Town, as long as the local non-white colleges do not provide facilities. The argument is, therefore, not based on fact and is bolstered by sentiment. But let me say that I have always been against excluding Bantu students from white universities. I do, however, welcome Bantu colleges as a needed supplement.

Now what is the difference between Smuts's mature attitude and the present rigid demarcation on lines of race? Smuts's philosophy of life was the Greek view, starting from Heracleitus—the view that life is something growing and expanding, to which we have to adapt ourselves without losing fundamental principles. Dogmatic formulations cut away the essential meaning, the manifold graciousness, the thing of many colours indicated in the New Testament.

On the subject of African majority rule, we may be sure that Oom Jannie would not have agreed to a counting of heads. He would have taken a stand on the different grades of development, and insisted on some means by which a test could be applied, if such a test is possible. He saw the point of Jung that culture is the real standard of difference, not colour. And culture means more than acquisition of a technical skill in modern society. It is in the depths of the unconscious, and formative in our development. It is the basis of human personality, of enormous importance in judgments of value. Very often ideals for society and the state are admirable, but are not practicable at a particular time. As Smuts repeatedly told us, there can be no absolute rigidity in political or social thinking. We cannot build stone walls between groups of people and expect them to last in perpetuity.

Today race problems have moved away from the English-Afrikaner relation and assumed sinister proportions in the White and non-White question. For the Afrikaner masses, who believe that their heritage is still in danger, this change has come too abruptly. They are encouraged in their fears by party leaders, who use the language and culture theme as a bogey. They are still concerned with the stock question; Do you want your sister to marry a 'kaffir'?—as if either the sister or the African would desire that. The approach is disquietingly negative—fear, fear, fear. A positive facing of the situation in a Christian spirit, recognition that the Bantu, the Coloured, the Indian, are fellow South Africans, whose help can be won by constructive citizenship, is ignored. The New Testament, in which there are positive examples of the association of different races, and the prayer of the Founder of Christianity for His followers 'that they all may be one', are pushed aside. The exciting experience of creating new friendships with people of different races and learning something in the process, is inhibited by the dogmatic assertion of differentiation as the will of God. What a dismal hopelessness!

This view is wrong—just as wrong as the theory of 'one man, one vote', which ignores different stages of development in the name of the power of the ballot-box.

Chapter VIII

SMUTS, KRUGER AND HIS ENGLISH
FRIENDS

Few things reveal the scale on which Smuts thought so vividly as his relationship with Paul Kruger, whose life he meant to write. Smuts knew all the sophistications of Europe, was consulted by Prime Ministers, consorted with Royalty; yet he retained to the end his abiding respect and affection for this son of the veld, Oom Paul. He realised his insight and natural wisdom, his uprightness and genuine piety. President Kruger could see possibilities in Smuts, and he could see through the machinations of party politicians and newspaper editors. When Professor Moorrees, the greatest of our preachers, went to see him at the time imperialism was rampant, just before the outbreak of the Anglo-Boer War, Oom Paul said: 'If you can stop the newspapers and Milner for six months, war can be avoided'. He was a natural Colossus, and he had wisdom founded on an intimate understanding of the Bible. Smuts, in spite of all his Cambridge culture, could appreciate that. He could see past the simplicity and occasional primitiveness of the old president. Between them there was a bond of affection and loyalty, which people in Europe could not always understand.

Smuts realised where his roots were. He knew that men like himself were often regarded in England as magnificent barbarians; so he said to a friend of mine in Oxford; magnificent in what they do and say, but not quite 'pukka'. They are 'barbarians' to the exclusive set. A person, like Smuts, who sees beyond the narrower concerns of his own people, and is criticised by them, often meets the judgment 'even his own people rejected him'; and co-operation, given on principle, is greeted with: 'now we regard you as one of us; you can be proud to call yourself an Englishman'. *Mutatis mutandis*, what we want of the English-born settler is that he should become a South African, while retaining his appreciation of English culture. It is hard for many people to understand a land of two European languages and two European cultures, contemplating a whole in which injustice is not done to either group, both being enriched by a generous, constructive Holism.

'In a little masterpiece of patriotic writing,' says Hancock (I. 148), 'he (Smuts) recorded a talk which he had had in April 1901 with a courageous Boer woman, who was able in her greatness of soul to show understanding even for a traitor.' In this essay upon Boer patriotism Smuts affirmed his passionate love for the soil of South Africa, 'the unbuilt country coming virgin from the hands of God'. . . . 'The city-dwellers who spoke English', he declared, 'could never love South Africa with the same understanding and self-surrender as belonged, by country and upbringing, to the country-dwelling Boers.' This was said at the time of the South African War. Yet nobody could have been more cordial to friends in England, or more co-operative with men of different nationalities, than Jan Christiaan Smuts. That was, indeed, the subject of complaint from men of a narrow nationalism.

Smuts has so often been characterised as an English imperialist that we should bear in mind other statements, such as the speech on the 16th December, Voortrekker

Day, in the year before his death, 1949. He was the only surviving Boer general, and he allowed his thoughts to go back into the past in which his emotions were deeply rooted. He saw himself again serving under Paul Kruger. He visualised the Afrikaner advancing, despite many difficulties and mistakes, under the guidance of Heaven. He dwelt on the sufferings of the Voortrekkers and on the elements of co-operation that alleviated their struggle. English settlers helped them when they set out in the Eastern Province. English blood flowed with theirs against Dingaan. Coloured and African servants stood by them and fell with them. They battled against war-lords, not against the Bantu people as a whole. They fought to find a peaceful home for their children, not to exterminate the natives.

When we look beyond the moves and counter-moves of party politics, the character of Paul Kruger stands out like a solid rock. In his scholarly book, *The Fall of Kruger's Republic*, J. S. Marais says about him: 'A born leader of men, Kruger had grown up with the State—a man of law and order, a conciliator also and a man of peace, but not peace at any price. It was he who struck hard in 1864, so as to bring the civil disturbances to a close. He went twice to London to negotiate, and only after it had become clear that the British government—or rather two successive British governments—were determined to maintain the annexation, did he take up arms, with the burghers united behind him. . . . *With the passage of time his stature grows steadily*' (my italics).

Marais referred to Paul Kruger as a colossal figure and quoted his last message: 'to take from the past the good that it contained and use it for building up the future'. The past contains, for us, not only conflict and destruction, but also a building-up, an Act of Union, the building of bridges, a whole-making activity between Englishman and Afrikaner, which should be extended step by step to embrace the different races in the country—an enormous task, but one worth attempting on the grounds of political principle.

It might be fitting to recall Kruger's estimate of Smuts, still in his twenties, upon his appointment as State Attorney in 1898. 'Smuts is one of the cleverest lawyers in South Africa, and also a man of versatile attainments. He is personally a very simple man, and meeting him one would not suspect that he possesses so iron a will and so determined a character as he does.' Although scarcely thirty years of age, and without the slightest experience of military affairs, Smuts developed in the later phases of the war into a brilliant general, adding to his position of State Attorney that of Assistant Commandant-General of the South African Republic. 'Smuts will yet play a great part (President Kruger truly prophesied) in the future history of South Africa' (*Memoirs of Paul Kruger*, Fisher Unwin, 1902).

In Smuts's group of English friends (we might also write Friends, because they were all Quakers or in close agreement with the Society) the Christian values of neighbourly love were sincerely felt and practised. But by the politicians they were classed as 'impractical idealists'. The 'inner light' Smuts shared with the Quakers told him that, in the long run, when all the party politicians had aired their views, the deeper insight would come from spiritual sources, although its value would not be realised immediately, in practice.

Another of Smuts's friends was Emily Hobhouse. Her name became a household word in the home of my grandfather at Paarl; he was for twenty-seven years an M.P. (M.L.A. then), and a staunch member of Hofmeyr's Bond, but also a personal friend of Cecil Rhodes. I remember the picture of her, wearing a large Victorian hat, at the time when the Boer generals, on their way to Europe, visited the house. Later, in 1914, when J. H. Hofmeyr, my contemporary, was staying with his mother in Museum Street, Oxford, Emily Hobhouse was in the vicinity. My contact with her was the cause she stood for, which she shared with the Gilletts—Margaret Gillett was a granddaughter of the redoubtable John Bright. Emily Hobhouse was tireless in her efforts to help those who were oppressed by imperialists and militarists. She was a grand figure, and Afrikaners will never forget what she did for the women and children. Wedding-presents were sold by the Gilbert Murrays after the war in aid of the same cause, and Margaret Gillett came to South Africa to give long and devoted practical help. Smuts felt a deep debt of gratitude to these women.

After Emily Hobhouse's eight years of voluntary work in the Transvaal, during which she helped the Boer women to spin, dye and weave the wool grown on the farms, Smuts paid a tribute to her that came from the depths of his being. At the monument in Bloemfontein in 1908 he presented her with a portrait of herself, painted by Hugo Naudé. When the Commemoration Monument to the women and children who died in the Concentration Camps was unveiled on 16th December 1913, Emily Hobhouse was unable to be present because of illness, but her speech was circulated. It was in memory of 26,370 women and children and 1,421 old men. Emily Hobhouse remembered Euripides, and quoted from the *Trojan Women* in Gilbert Murray's translation, the words of the prophetess Cassandra, on Athenian imperialism and the sufferings of the women:

> 'Would ye be wise, ye cities, fly from war!
> Yet if war come, there is a crown in death
> For her that striveth well and perisheth
> Unstained.'

She believed, like Edith Cavell in later times, that 'Patriotism is not enough: there must be no hatred in my heart'. The following were her actual words: 'Alongside of the honour we pay the sainted dead, forgiveness must find a place. I have read that when Christ said, "Forgive your enemies", it was not only for the sake of the enemy He said so, but for one's own sake, 'because love is more beautiful than hate'. Surely your dead with the wisdom that now is theirs, know this. To harbour hate is fatal to your own self-development. It makes a flaw, for hatred like rust, eats into the soul of a nation as of an individual.

'As you bring your tribute to the dead, bury untor-giveness and bitterness at the foot of this monument forever. Instead, forgive, for you can afford it, the rich who were greedy for more riches, the statesmen who could not guide affairs, the bad generalship that warred on weaklings and babes—forgive, because so only can you rise to full nobility of character and a broad and noble national life.

'For what really matters is *character*. History clearly teaches this.

'In the present day, minds are strangely confused, eyes are blinded, and it is the almost universal idea that the all-important thing for a country is material prosperity. It is false.

'For it is not the rich and prosperous who matter

77

most, but you who live the simplest lives and upon whom in the last resort, if trial comes, falls the test of national character.

'The honour of a country . . . lies in the sum-total of her best traditions, which the people at large will rise up to maintain.'

'Even as the noblest men are ever ready to admit and remedy an error, so England, as soon as she was convinced of the wrong being done in her name to the weak and defenceless, confessed it *in very deed*, and by thorough reformation of those camps rendered them fit for human habitation.'

Emily Hobhouse looked back to the Greek scene. familiar to Smuts; she also referred to the famous oration of Pericles:

'True it is of your dead, that which Pericles said of his countrymen: "The grandest of all sepulchres they have, not that in which mortal bones are laid, but a home in the minds of men; their story lives on far away, without visible symbol, woven into the stuff of other men's lives".'

When Emily Hobhouse died in 1926 her ashes were brought to South Africa and buried at the foot of the monument. Thus she atoned, and atonement is etymologically at-one-ment, harmony, co-operation, Wholeness.

Emily Hobhouse found a deep echo in the heart of Smuts. But as an administrator he was faced with the problem of applying fine principles in an imperfect and fragmentary world, which had barely glimpsed the meaning of Holism.

Smuts spoke in Hollands at the unveiling of the Monument:

'When one remembers that the whole population of the Republic, man, woman and child, probably did not number many more than two hundred thousand souls, then one realises the terrible, overwhelming meaning of these figures (the numbers who died). What misery, what anxiety of soul must have filled the hearts of most of these women in those dreadful days! And yet, we who remained in the field know that, from the women's side, with a few exceptions, no attempt was ever made to persuade the men to surrender. These women were indeed worthy descendants of their brave mothers and grandmothers. . . . For those among us who recognise in the long list the names of wives, mothers, daughters and children—and many of us do so—great self-control and austerity is demanded to rid oneself of all feelings of bitterness. We are profoundly moved and our throats tighten when we remember everything . . . and yet I say it is our duty to cherish no bitterness or hate. We may and we must teach our children to try to be worthy of such mothers . . . The bloodshed in our past is not one of the things upon which we must fashion our future . . . must we not believe that it is God's will that we try to walk another road: the road of love and peace?'

Here we see the heart of Jan Christiaan Smuts meeting the kindred spirit of Emily Hobhouse, and the Wholeness of that conception renews our hope for the future.

President Kruger's last message was given in Clarens, Switzerland, on the 29th June, 1904, and sent in a letter to General Botha. I quote from D. W. Kruger's Biography of the President (II. 298) and express my thanks to Professor P. J. van der Merwe of the University of Stellenbosch for his valuable help in a matter over which some confusion has arisen. The reader should compare with Professor Kruger's the account of Oom Paul in *Die Groot Gryse*, by Anna M. Louw, recently published.

Shortly before his death Paul Kruger had received evidence of a new political life in the Transvaal. A congress of the people, led by General Botha, took place from 23rd to 25th May 1904, and a unanimous resolution was passed to send greetings to Kruger, and express sorrow that he could not receive this greeting in his own country. In his accompanying letter Botha told him that people were beginning to realise that only by unity could they stand as a nation. Kruger felt that a special reply was required, and asked Bredell and Leyds to compose on his behalf a suitable message that could be used for publication. This was the origin of the letter that Leyds terms a kind of 'political testament'. The President accepted Leyds's draft with a few additions. His longing to return was constant, but the hope of realising it was faint. In its final form this letter, the last to be signed by Kruger, read as follows:

Dear General (Botha),

It is a great privilege to be able to acknowledge your cable of 25th May and your letter of the 29th of the same month, bringing me the greetings of the Congress held in Pretoria, 23 to 25 May, 1904. (Kruger died in July of that year.)

Amid the sorrow and suffering that have fallen to my lot, this greeting made me grateful to you.

With all my heart I thank all those gathered together to take counsel for the present and the future, that they gave a thought to their old State President and so showed that they had not forgotten the past.

For those who want to create a future must not lose sight of the past.

Therefore my message is this: SEEK IN THE PAST ALL THE GOOD AND THE BEAUTIFUL

THAT CAN BE FOUND IN IT, AND FORM YOUR IDEAL ACCORDINGLY, AND TRY FOR THE FUTURE TO REALISE THAT IDEAL.

It is true that much that was built up is now destroyed, spoiled, fallen. But by unity of purpose and unity of strength, that which at present is overthrown can be built up again.

I am moved to gratitude also to see that this unity, this harmony prevails with you. Always remember the serious warning contained in the words 'divide and rule', and see to it that this saying may never become applicable to the Afrikaans people.

Then our national feeling and our language will continue to flourish. What I myself shall live to see of this, rests in the hand of God.

Born under the English flag, I have no desire to die under it.

I have learned to find contentment in the bitter thought that I shall close my eyes as an exile in a strange land, almost totally alone, far from relations and friends whom I shall probably never see again, far from the Afrikaans territory on which I shall perhaps never set foot again, far from the land to which I devoted my life, to open it up for civilisation, and where I see my own people developing into a nation.

But the bitterness will be alleviated as long as I may cherish the conviction that the work that was begun is being continued.

For then the hope and expectation that in the end that work will prosper, continues to support me. May it be so!

From the depth of my heart I greet the whole people.

(This document was signed)   S. J. P. KRUGER.

For Smuts the experience represented by his life in Parliament and in the Party, in spite of its necessary human contacts, could be very trying, and often seemed almost futile. More than once he wondered if any great things could be achieved in this way. If this had been all, he would have been discouraged and frustrated. But it was not all. Just as professors feel, beyond the routine of university organisation, a deep interest in the things taught, a love for the subject studied, a readiness to devote their lives to it, Smuts had a profound human interest in men and their affairs and values.

One of these values, as we have seen, was his view of life, his philosophy of the Whole, an interest which began with his student days. He discussed it with his great friend, Wolstenholme, the Cambridge don, who represented the academic approach. Smuts had something in his outlook that the academic could not quite grasp. On 12th March 1912, Wolstenholme wrote to Oom Jannie from Cambridge: 'Your method is that of speculative metaphysics, and runs riot—like Bergson's—in the "hypostatization of abstracts", which to me is Anathema Maranatha. '(*Anathema* was the curse pronounced against a man who professed to be a Christian, but had no personal loyalty to Christ.)[1]

Wolstenholme proceeds: 'Your Holism is but one presentation of a metaphysical neo-vitalism, similar to, but still bolder than, that of Driesch . . . but has little chance of being accepted in any metaphysical form. Your philosophizing . . . is metaphysical from the outset. I hold by science and scientific method; but I mean by science

[1] *Maranatha*—even the correct way of writing the word is a matter of dispute among scholars—seems to mean 'Come O Lord' a liturgical cry, transliterated from the Aramaic—I Corinthians 16, 22—See Peake, *Commentary on the Bible*, 1962.

all knowledge.' Smuts's conception of 'intensive' knowledge Wolstenholme in the main rejected. (*Smuts Papers*,
III. p. 67ff.) Wolstenholme believed that Smuts was
following a delusion in holding that the Universe has a
meaning or purpose, and he urged him to confine himself
to the facts of history. Smuts had all the technical equip-
ment and could hold his own with Wolstenholme in
learned discussion. But he also had something simpler
and deeper. He thought that our ancient spiritual heir-
looms need not be ruthlessly scrapped. 'Beauty and
holiness are as much aspects of Nature as energy and
entropy; they belong to the unutterable mysteries of the
Universe.' Smuts recalled the synoptic vision of Plato:
'Holism is an attempt at Synthesis . . . not a system of
philosophy. I don't believe very much in systems.
Science has proved the greatest constructive force in the
world, but also . . . the greatest destructive agent.' Nor
did Smuts understand the Bible in the orthodox manner;
he thought of Christ as the greatest Personality in history.

While he was still at Stellenbosch and not yet twenty,
he composed Spenserian stanzas to Isie Krige, his future
wife, on her nineteenth birthday, the idea being to discover a unity between the seen and the unseen, and to
help Isie to understand this. His humanism found further
expression in an essay, entitled *Homo Sum*, which included
a discussion on *Eenheid* and its relation to law and human
personality. He read great writers like Whitman, who
had tried to conceive of life as whole.

This fundamental and life-long concern with Wholeness shows that Smuts did not take up Holism in order to
bolster his political outlook. Rather, he saw local
problems in terms of a larger Destiny that was shaping
the events of the world.

Carl Jung wrote: 'Matter contains the seed of spirit and spirit the seed of matter.' Whatever meaning we may now give to these terms, Dr. Morgenthau of Yale, a modern scientist, believes that matter exists as purpose. Smuts certainly believed in an end towards which objects in Nature develop. But was the end planned by a Power standing outside natural law, outside the three-dimensional world, a Divine Agency, or was it a matter of natural selection and evolution?

It seems to me that Smuts, speaking in the company of fellows scientists, spoke of teleology as an evolutionary factor, as he does in his book on Holism; but later, when he began to feel that his book needed revision, he inclined to the other explanation, a Divine ordering of the Universe and a Planner behind the Plan.

To gain clarity on this point we should therefore look, not to what Smuts said about science, but to what he said about religion in its broader implications; for there was, as Monsignor Kolbe said, a profoundly religious element in Smuts. 'Throughout his life,' says Hancock (I. 114) 'Smuts kept returning to this idea: that God in working out his purposes, calls upon men to work with Him.' Towards the close of the South African War he penned a remarkable despatch. According to Hancock, 'he stormed the British camp, beat off a counter-attack launched by General Cunningham with 2,500 men, and inflicted heavy casualties on the enemy. . . . The British forces, he reported to Botha, had been wholly driven from the Gatsrand; the Boer commandos, so recently a rabble, had fought splendidly. *It was a notable sign of God's guidance* (I. 125, my italics). In August 1901, before the invasion of the Cape Colony, Smuts addressed the troops: this war (he said) was not only a struggle for the Afrikaner people;

it was a struggle for right, for God. If they failed, God would fail too. . . . He who loved his life more than the right was unworthy to be a man or a burgher.' Here, perhaps, we may detect the note of the orator and the emotion of the occasion; but behind it is an element that represents the soul of Smuts. At the end of the war, he said the war of freedom for South Africa had been fought, not only for Boers, but for the entire people. 'The result of that struggle we leave in God's hands. Perhaps it is His will to lead the people of South Africa, through defeat and humiliation, yes, even through the valley of the shadow of death, to a better future and a brighter day.' There was no insincerity in this picture; it is typical of Smuts, the man of vision.

'Let us do our duty according to our best lights and leave the ultimate issue to that Providence which somehow turns evil to good, and makes poor erring humanity reap "the far-off interest of tears".' (*Hancock* I. 378.) So he wrote to Arthur Gillett at the beginning of the First World War. There is no rhetoric here. To Isie, with equal sincerity, he wrote about this time: 'Mankind is in a terrible state and stretches out it hands for help and rescue. God alone can rescue, but all can help.' To the Gilletts he wrote about the sad state of central Europe: 'What will Northcliffe and Bottomley and Beelzebub say? Ah, yes, and what will God say? For there is the rub.' In 1918 Smuts wrote to Alice Clark, with whom he always got down to fundamentals, 'I do believe the Lord is really on the move. I only hope that in moving to meet Him we may not make the wrong move. For Satan is also on the move.' (*Hancock* I. 470.) In 1940 he wrote to Margaret Gillett: 'Man has no abiding city except in the Eternal, however we picture it to ourselves. . . . The universe must be seen as the organic structure that it is, instinct with Divinity, big with the inner spirit that is shaping and creating it, and of which it is but the progressive expression.'

Smuts was big enough to appreciate values as well as scientific analysis: 'The measureable is always the least important aspect of it (Nature). . . . One has to read Newton's *Principia* together with Wordsworth's *Prelude* and *Tintern Abbey* in order to get some vague idea of the real truth.' The deepest truth, for him, was that of the spirit not the intellect.

As he became older Smuts moved more and more towards the truth, as he saw it; there must be a rebirth in the individual, a new realisation of values. 'The situation is at bottom a religious problem. . . . How can we picture the Highest, which would absorb all our love and passionate devotion, and make our hearts once more burn in us as did the vision of Jesus to the two disciples of Emmaus?' (Letter to Margaret Gillett, 1945.) There is intense earnestness in these words.

Paradoxically, there was a streak of ruthlessness in Oom Jannie, which certain critics, for instance, the writer of *Grey Steel*, exploited. His military duties sometimes clashed with human feeling and made him unpopular with the masses. There were undoubted cases where Smuts the humanist was pushed aside by Smuts the general. Yet when Emily Hobhouse pleaded for General de Wet, Smuts listened to her. Most of the rebels of 1915 received a reprieve; justice was tempered with mercy.

Smuts, from 1914 to 1919, was regarded as the foremost leader in Europe, and his advice at imperial conferences was treated with the greatest respect. Yet in South Africa feeling against him, after the 1922 strike, was such that his life was in danger. Leaders in Britain said: 'Europe needs him. His work in Africa is done. His future belongs to the world.'

Clearly, there are three different aspects of Smuts's whole-making vision; as a statesman:

(1) He tried to build bridges between South Africa and Britain, a formidable task, in view of the recent experiences of the Afrikaners;
(2) He tried to bridge the gulf between the English and Afrikaans elements in South Africa; the adoption of the Act of Union bears testimony to his zeal in this direction;
(3) He tried to work out a co-operative basis for the relation of Whites and non-Whites, but did not get much beyond a theory.

As an ambassador of South African interests in Britain, he was by far the best man for the work. He had a natural capacity for persuading people, and exercised it to a higher degree in Europe than he did among his own people in South Africa. Circumstances there gave him his opportunity, and he made skilful use of his chances. Kitchener's early hint to him about the probable advent of a Liberal Government proved very important, and provided a turning point in British-South African post-war negotiations. He could not identify himself to a large extent with British policy; and he pointed out that all his life he had striven for the principle of liberty, as opposed to the repressive politics of men like Milner. He seemed to fit naturally into the British context, and was more and more given positions of trust and authority. He was later tentatively offered a position in the British Cabinet. He found everywhere congenial colleagues: Sir Harold

Nicolson, on one of his missions to Central Europe, said about Smuts: 'a delightful man, telling us stories of the veld with a ring of deep home-sickness in his voice. A lovely man. Our rations are even more Spartan than before. . . .' He seemed to make friends easily, and to achieve much understanding from similar aims for the peace of the world; overseas, he was away from the smallness, suspicions and frustrations of party-politics—to him, a welcome relief. Nobody could have done more for good relations between Britain and South Africa. Smuts was in his holistic element.

Chapter IX

THE LIFE OF THE SPIRIT

Smuts did a great deal to modify the patronizing air that was prominent in Britain and South Africa in his time, and has not died out yet. Anglo-Saxons do not say openly 'we are superior'; but an 'inner circle' in the Clubs act impliedly on that basis. Louis Leipoldt, who tried to feel at home in both cultures, and was in fact a very good South African, had personal knowledge of the English tradition and sentiment, yet he was sometimes looked at askance by the clubmen, because they thought he lacked the veneer. In the development of South Africanism, Leipoldt was more far-seeing than either the narrow Afrikaner Nationalist, or the single-culture English South African. Even in this country people find it hard to understand the man of two languages and cultures. After a press attack on me, an Englishman said: 'But we think of you as one of us—as one of the cultural leaders.' My reply was: 'I am an Afrikaner, with a strong feeling for the Afrikaans tradition, but also for the tradition of England, to which Afrikaners owe a great deal. I try to be a South African.'

But our hearts are small, as Kipling said; consequently we are limited in our loyalties. The heart of Smuts was not small. His expanding interest in problems of unity started at Stellenbosch, with the conception of Eenheid, which applied particularly to the Boers in their struggle against imperialism. The new prospect opened up by Kitchener induced him to extend it to imperial problems, which, as he saw it, included the development of South Africa. Finally, he was genuinely concerned with the peace of Europe and the world. But in the technique of party politics, this breadth was mistaken for opportunism. Unity and freedom, to Smuts, were fundamental. Behind the party game he was concerned with lasting values of a moral nature, and these were largely stimulated by his Friends at 102 Banbury Road, and their associates. To understand Smuts we must look not alone at the party methods, which he regarded as inevitable and found extremely boring.

Contact with people faced with dire practical situations, and a magnetic and courageous personality, enabled Smuts to kindle optimism even though he himself felt hopeless. There was in him the kind of resurgent life that helped him to survive many droughts of the spirit. The inner life, not dependent on external factors or material help, was his finest characteristic, the real source of his faith and his amazingly buoyant strength. It surprised all his colleagues.

I remember once going to the offices of the various Ministers in the Union Buildings, towards Christmas time. All were deserted, because the Ministers had begun their holidays—all except two: the offices of J. H. Hofmeyr, another prodigious worker, and the office of Smuts. They demanded hard work and austerity from subordinates, but they themselves set the example. One could excuse a certain hardness, unjustly called ruthlessness, in Smuts, under the compulsion of practical politics. The world was not ready for Wholeness, unable to look beyond immediate gain, unable to ignore the small grievance for the generous co-operation, unwilling to try to make Wholes out of discordant fragments.

The harmony denied by most men was recovered by Smuts in communion with Nature. This was not a sentiment, but a genuine experience. His feeling for Table Mountain linked up with his feeling for Doornkloof and his love of reading Wordsworth's *Prelude*. There was strength in it, more stability than he found in the milling masses of men around him. It gave him a sense of fundamental values. It was an inspiration and a help, physically and mentally. His lonely walks on Table Mountain meant associating with a living friend. 'The mountains uphold us, and the stars beckon to us.' He told Margaret Gillett that his Mountain oration was a bit of himself, 'not merely a speech.' He spoke of the spirit of Nature blending with the spirit of man. The mountain was his ladder of the soul; 'from it came the Law, from it came the Gospel in the Sermon on the Mount'. It conferred a new freedom, remote from the petty worries in the valley, a new exhilaration and a kinship with the great creative Spirit. But we must learn to practise the religion of the mountain down in the valley also.

This lyrical language showed that Smuts's experience reached great depths of perception. Wherever they travelled, his private secretary told me, he found time to study the phenomena of Nature. 'I don't forget my grasses,' he said. Nor did he in his speech forget his companions of the First World War:

'Here for a thousand years their memory shall blend with the great rock masses and humanise them. . . . All moral and spiritual values are expressed in terms of altitude and the metaphors embedded in Language reflect the realities of progress. . . . The religion of the Mountain is, in reality, the religion of joy, of the release of the soul from the thoughts that weigh it down and fill it with a sense of sorrow and defeat.' Smuts's whole view of evolution in Nature was that it stood for the evolution of the spirit.

Here, then, was a sickly child, who had no schooling until he was twelve, and for whose development there seemed no bright prospects. Suddenly, impelled by an inner force, he shot ahead and obtained a double First at Cambridge. His period with Kruger put him in the anti-British camp. He understood the meaning and the pathos of Oom Paul's words to the imperialists: 'It is not the franchise, it is my country that you want.' When later he did fight for a changed interpretation of the conception of empire, he was consistent in his principles. On the 11th April 1917, during the First World War, he said 'the cause I fought for fifteen years ago is the cause I am fighting for today. I fought for liberty and freedom then, and I am fighting for them today.'

England suddenly discovered Smuts, but a Smuts very different from his early history. The extensiveness of his achievement—his settlement of strikes, his re-organisation of the Air Force in Britain, his work for South Africa at the Peace Conference, his conception of a Commonwealth of independent nations to supersede the old idea of empire, his building of the League of Nations and its successor, UNO, his work for the establishment of a South African outlook (whatever party opponents may say)—all these marked steps forward that conservatives in Britain often shuddered to behold; but they proved constructive.

In May 1917, Smuts said: 'If you ask me what is wrong with Europe, I should say the moral basis of Europe, the bedrock of the Christian moral code, has become undermined and can no longer support all that superstructure of economic and industrial prosperity, which the last century has built upon it, and the vast whole is now sagging.'

He distinguished between the old German culture that he knew, and the Prussian perversion that came in his time (June 1917). 'All Germans, but the Prussians, have been a peaceful people always. But either from Frederick the Great or from Napoleon the Prussians learnt a devilish lesson.'

Smuts himself, says Sarah Gertrude Millin, liked the Germans better than the French. He did not, however, like the extremism of many Continentals at the Peace Conference, and deplored their savage fighting for spoils. They repudiated the fourteen points of Wilson—as America itself was induced to do. The British people had given pledges concerning their war aims, made public by Lloyd George in January 1918, and reaffirmed in September of that year. 'For myself,' said Smuts, 'I have always looked upon these declarations as bedrock, as governing any peace treaty which would be made at the end of the war.' (Sarah Getrude Millin, *General Smuts* II. 236 ff.)

'A consideration of the document on its merits,' said Smuts of the peace terms later, 'shows it will make a bad peace. It is not just, and it cannot be durable. Many of the terms are impossible to carry out. They will produce political and economic chaos in Europe for a generation, and in the long run it will be the British Empire that will have to pay the penalty. . . . This Treaty has been called an English peace, but it is nothing of the sort. The military occupation of a large part of industrial Germany for fifteen years is indefensible, from every point of view.... *The roots of war are in the document* (my italics). . . . When aggression comes . . . the British Empire will be called up to jump in.' Oom Jannie could see the roots of Nazi dictatorship; but the delegates to the Conference, blinded with emotion, could not see.

Smuts realised the meaning of *poikilos* (I *Peter* 4:10) 'the *manifold* grace of God' (implying much more than *multiformis* in the Latin Bible), the rich and changing colours on the sunlit back of a pigeon. The ever-changing quality of life calls to us to appreciate its depth and variety, without sacrifice to our principles. Truth looks in more ways than one. It has adaptability, it has humour. It is alive. These qualities seem to escape unimaginative men at the Conference-table, obsessed with practical interests that turn out to be so impractical in the long run. General Smuts knew this only too well; and he was often forced to exclaim: 'How long, O Lord, how long?'

CHAPTER X

OXFORD SOCIETY

During his return to South Africa on board the Edinburgh Castle, Smuts wrote: 'My mind kept moving between the two great circles of Doornkloof and 102 (Banbury Road, Oxford). There was no conflict between the two.'

Smuts was trained at Cambridge, but the deepest development of his thought took place at Oxford. The house at 102 Banbury Road was the home of Arthur Gillett and his wife Margaret; it had associations, too, with Margaret's sister, Alice Clark, and with Oom Jannie's daughter Cato, who became Mrs. Bancroft Clark. Emily Hobhouse often came there and many forward-looking Friends (in the sense of Quakers). South Africans, like myself, had tea there on a Sunday afternoon, and often went to the Quaker Meeting with the Gilletts, among them my future wife Jessie. There were many Liberals like dear Gilbert Murray, whose home on Boar's Hill, 'Yatscombe,' was always open to us; his translations of Euripides, which moderns affect to despise, were read at 102 Banbury Road, and warmly appreciated.

Oxford had ubiquitous connections; between different kinds of people, between widely varying themes; it found the significant links. Another leader whom we recall with affection was Canon Streeter of Queen's, famous for his international study-groups. To Oom Jannie Oxford was spiritual recreation. He got away from the wrangles of politics, both in Britain and in South Africa; he played with the children and loved it; he made contact with his godson, Jan Gillett, who shared his interest in Botany, and is now Head of the Herbarium in Nairobi. Smuts loved the gracious atmosphere of 102 Banbury Road, as many of us came to love it; he also found rest and strength and common moral interests. There was a perfect Whole, a harmony of the scientific and the human.

It was borne in upon thinking people there that, in order to survive, man must consider not only the ethics of war, but its total prevention. The driving force must come from the hearts of people, such as the Quakers at Oxford. Simplicity, honesty, love, were the qualities needed, and Smuts admired all those who genuinely stood for them. 'It is the religion of pity that we most need today. Power, science, economics, these are three things most frequently emphasised in our world. But Paul's Three—the real Big Three—I see little of.' Those who doubt Smuts's religious feeling should read his words uttered at this time. Banbury Road and Doornkloof—two centres of peace and strength. 'I almost feel reborn in this atmosphere of peace' he wrote about Doornkloof.

Because Smuts did not agree with the dogma of belief in the organised churches, he was not irreligious. He always proclaimed his assent to fundamental principles of Christianity. A dedicated churchman like Monsignor Kolbe, with his customary insight, could realise that in Smuts's *Holism and Evolution* there was a conception of organic structure, informed by a living spirit of growth and creativeness.

Smuts thought that the action of mind and spirit cannot be contained within Professor Hogben's terms of physics and chemistry, because science does not cover all the facts of experience, and neglects the importance of values. It cannot explain the immense impact of human personality. Scholars such as Gilbert Murray, J. A. Smith, A. D. Lindsay, John MacMurray and J. S. Haldane, supported Smuts in general principle. But many philosophers, terrified of being dubbed metaphysicians, rejected *Holism and Evolution*. A prominent exception was R. G. Collingwood, whose standing among his colleagues was high.

In his letters to and discussions with friends at Oxford, Smuts often showed prophetic insight: 'I sometimes fear that this war' (he wrote in 1919) 'is simply the vanguard of calamity, and that the Great Horror is still to come. It is an awful thought, that the great storm has not merely blown off the rotten and weak branches of the human tree, but affected the tree itself, and that in future it will for generations have only stunted growth. I believe in God and I believe in Good. But, dear Alice, I am often very low and despondent over it all. Only a few years ago we still saw the vision of the New Earth. In Paris that vision vanished. And now arises that other vision of human decay, when God rings down the curtain, and darkness settles down once more on human destiny. What is in store for us all? . . . Have we passed through one great historic cycle, and are we entering upon a very different one—perhaps much worse?' (*Hancock* II. 10).

Alice Clark felt for him, and tried to encourage him to do the immediate duty 'knowing that God is good and is all.' Smuts replied, 'I think of you and of the sources of Goodness and Power in the nature of the Whole. You have already assimilated the central idea of Holism. . . . The Goodness of God and the existence of Evil still remain the great religious and metaphysical problem. And we shall never solve it theoretically, because as partial beings we cannot grasp the whole where these antinomies disappear. . . . Unless society is to go to pieces, there must be the solid guarantee of force in the background, and this will remain so until human nature has undergone a thorough change.'

Looking back on his activities Smuts thought that politics was no life for a Christian. This inner thought which he shared with Alice Clark and the others at Oxford seems to me the real Smuts.

Men of vision can often see too far ahead, and fail to understand the immediate cares of the ordinary man. About politics, Smuts once confessed humbly: 'We have to labour on with our little palliatives and keep the show going with some appearance of human decency.' To Margaret he said, 'Arthur (her husband) finds the trouble in the world beyond him and falls back more and more on the philosophy of home life. The greatest and truest of all philosophies in my humble opinion. It only shows that Arthur is wiser than I and others who toil at problems beyond our powers. And yet what can one do? Is it possible for those who occupy positions of leadership to fold their hands and admit defeat?'

A consistent trend in Smuts's thought grew in association with his Oxford Friends and formed the basis of his philosophy of life. He was thrown back, in the last resort, on religion, which cannot be separated from our search for truth.

The invincible optimism of Oom Jannie, his delight in walks round the beautiful Oxford countryside, his appreciation of the Oxford don who always saw the

humorous side, even in the depths of war; all this light-
ened the conversation at 102 Banbury Road, to which the
resilience of Oom Jannie's spirit greatly contributed.

The humanism of Oxford was the making of a master
spirit.

Chapter XI

A VISION OF DANTE

1

After a conversation with Oom Jannie in Pretoria, when the complexities of party politics were pushed aside, I had a dream. It was more than usually vivid and seemed to penetrate to a deeper reality. It made me think of Dante's vision of Beatrice, though I do not wish to compare my experience with that of so exalted a poet! There was first the element of light, a radiant light in the surrounding darkness, such as was seen by Vergil, whom Dante chose as his guide.

> 'Thick as autumnal leaves that strow the brooks
> In Vallombrosa, where Etrurian shades
> High o'er-arched embower. . . .'

are the words with which Milton describes gloom.

It has been noted by Miss J. R. Bacon (*Classical Review* 53:3) that there is an increased and increasing use of words indicating *light* in the eighth book of the *Aeneid*, which foreshadows the work of Aeneas in Italy. There is progressive experience of light in both Vergil and Dante. It is associated with joy and truth. *Ex umbris et imaginibus in veritatem*, advance from shadows and phantoms to the realisation of truth. It is a radiant light that clothes the fields in Vergil's poem; in the *Paradiso* Dante described the vision of Beatrice as so glad that the very planet became brighter for it. 'O Lady,' says Dante, 'in

whom my hope has strength . . . guard your magnificence
in me, that my soul *which you have made whole*, may be
pleasing to you. . . .'

> 'So I prayed; and she, far away as she seemed,
> smiled (*sorrise*) as she looked on me.'

That smile symbolised the eventual attainment of inner
peace, after all the storms and frustrations of the material
world, the eventual atonement, through 'the Love that
moves the sun and the other stars' (*l'amor che move il sole e
l'altre stelle*).

Now this dream made a deep impression on me
because it was somehow associated with Jan Christiaan
Smuts. It seemed to me a symbol of his thought behind
all the bustle of external activities; the fountain of
inspiration that enabled him to keep up his strength, and
to smile despite countless discouragements.

It was a symbol of that concrete experience of friendship and communion realised in 102 Banbury Road,
Oxford, where we found so much spiritual encouragement. In my dream I saw Smuts accompanied by a
presence so radiant that I cannot hope to describe it—a
presence that offered strength and wisdom, deeper than
the abundance of books and learning.

Smuts tried to communicate his thoughts to Monsignor Kolbe and Professor J. I. Marais. He did so
imperfectly, and neither Kolbe nor Marais could fully
agree with Smuts's version of his beliefs. Wolstenholme,
his Cambridge friend, in England, could not bear to read
more than a small fragment of his philosophy. But both
Kolbe and Marais, from their different points of view,
realised that there was something bigger than the verbal
formulation of holistic ideas.

Smuts was concerned with the two great principles laid down by Jesus, summarising his teaching to mankind: 'love your neighbour' and 'love God'.

When the lawyer in the Gospel persisted: 'Who is my neighbour?' the answer came from Christ in the form of the parable of the Good Samaritan.

Now the city of Samaria, later called Sebaste (or Augusta as the Romans named it in honour of the Emperor), was in the centre of Palestine and the Samaritans were a mixed race, sprung from the union of Assyrian colonists and the remnants of the tribes of Ephraim and Manasseh, which were not carried away into Babylon. Strict Jews avoided Samaria and ceased to regard it as part of the Holy Land. The victim of the story was probably a Jew coming from Jerusalem, helped by a man of mixed race, who was scorned by orthodox religious people. It is this Samaritan's solicitude that is held up as an example by Jesus. And the answer given to the question 'who is my neighbour?' is 'the man who behaves like a neighbour to one who needs help, however different he may be in race and religious tradition.' A true neighbour does not ask whether the sufferer belongs to a particular set or not. The law of neighbourly love cuts clean across the divisions of society, and takes no notice of the tradition that 'the Jews have no dealings with the Samaritans.' This love, as Jesus saw it, is universal.

2

About the time Smuts returned to Cape Town (4th August 1919), he received a letter from Professor J. I. Marais, the aged theologian of Stellenbosch. I translate his High Dutch: 'I mourn over South Africa .... There is a kind of patriotism that humiliates, lowers, dishonours, because it is a reflection of egoism, selfishness, narrow-mindedness, separation and tearing apart. There is also, thank Heaven, a patriotism that enlightens, ennobles, blesses and does not curse. This is what I seek and I find it not, alas! in many of your opponents. May it be granted to you, in accordance with your peculiar experiences, to lead our South African patriotism on the right road, and to heal the breach that exists at present.'

Arrived in Pretoria, Smuts wrote to Margaret Gillett: 'The homecoming to Doornkloof was the best . . . Doornkloof was a dream.' He rejoiced exceedingly to be back in the South Africa he loved.

But his joy was shattered by the death of General Botha on 28th August 1919—a beloved colleague who had shared many difficult years with him—years that had been a test of faith as well as friendship.

'He was South Africa's greatest son, and, among men, my best friend.' That is how Smuts saw Louis Botha, and Alice Clark responded at once: 'Dear Jannie, what a grievous blow for thee' (at this solemn moment she reverts to the old Quaker form of address) 'and for many others . . . I know thou has for long realised that his life was precarious; but he was so young to be taken; one hoped there were many years left for him to serve the good cause—thou must now feel very much alone, for no one else can ever take the place which he has filled in thy life. 'Smuts was always fond of Goethe, and might have recalled the words of the poet: *Im Ganzen, im Guten, im Schoenen resolut zu leben*, 'to live steadfastly in the Whole, the Good and the Beautiful.'

Oxford took an interest in South Africa in those days, and we rejoiced in the universal spirit we found there. In our group we had people from Ceylon, Holland, South Africa, Australia, England, prematurely picturing an international world order. Alas for our hopes! The papers we presented for discussion are forgotten. But the personal links that were formed in Berlin and in Oxford were to last, and survived the upheaval of our time.

Oxford means many things to many people. To Smuts it meant the cultural link that, despite the distressing strife and misunderstanding of our world, binds together those who understand the meaning of *humanitas*, the art of civilised life.

Homo homini lupus, 'man to his fellow man is a wolf', How many leaders have experienced that! That was what General Louis Botha felt at the Paris peace conference. That was what Smuts of the inner values felt when faced by the demands of international politics, which claimed to be practical.

Milner thought himself the Englishman *par excellence*; but the values of Oxford never meant to him what they came to mean for Smuts. The capacity for understanding the minds of people was not found in Milner nor the imaginative sympathy. The outstanding fact, however, is that war produced no stable solution.

3

When the term Holism was drawn into the language of party politics, it was often abused and distorted. In Smuts's philosophy it is a tendency making for what is ethically harmonious, a fulfilment of potentialities of development. But in party politics it became a dogma of accomplished fact. It was therefore implied that Smuts excluded the right of South Africa to secede from the

Commonwealth. When this bond was eventually put to the electorate, the answer was an uncompromising NO.

Now this was not the conception of empire that had evolved in Smuts's thought. He had always stood for self-development and elasticity in imperial affairs. That was his principle. But Smuts was committed to play an active part in party-politics against his will, owing to a contempt for the machinations involved. Tielman Roos regarded politics as a game. Smuts did not, and he was often faced with a clash between political expediency and the principles in which he truly believed.

He had fought for South Africa's status at the peace conference and placed it on an equal footing with that of Britain. He claimed that South Africa had achieved a 'higher status', by becoming a member of the League of Nations. Many people doubted this. To Smuts, there was safety for South Africa in the wholeness of the British Empire and the privileges South Africa had gained by the very fact that the Empire remained an elastic and expanding institution, offering advantages in proportion as co-operation and understanding prevailed. The idea of the establishment of an Imperial Cabinet, on a permanent basis, was in the air. The old political ties were being revised. An empire on a new footing was coming into being, and Smuts saw advantages in this for South Africa. And so, at a time when many oversea politicians were willing to condone the right of secession, Smuts stood out against it, because of internal political pressures.

Yet he could have combined his conception of South African nationhood, for which he had fought many battles against the Imperialists, with an open door to the development of secession. His position was so strong in Europe, after all his services, that he could have persuaded the oversea politicians, and won over the opposition inside South Africa. Independent development, approached with care and wisdom, was a natural feature of the principle of growth within the Empire, and should not have become a means of inflaming racial hatred. The people needed education and encouragement, based on a positive love for South Africa. Smuts should have demonstrated that this love could be combined with the position of South Africa as an equal independent state within the Commonwealth.

Already the bogey of *fusion* was raising its head. The Afrikaner was not prepared to be 'fused'. He had struggled for many years to demonstrate his individuality, and the right to develop his own language. It had been a hard struggle, the cultural depth of which Smuts never understood, in his preoccupation with imperial policies. The Afrikaner, who had grown up with the 'superior attitude' of his English fellow-citizens in regard to his culture, and had listened to derogatory remarks about Afrikaans, was filled with fear that larger imperial contacts would lead to the swamping of the Afrikaner tradition. He believed that separate development, for that moment of time, was the only safe road for him. Smuts appeared to be going ahead too far and too fast.

If you want to convince people you must be able to enter into their feelings, and foster what is positive and whole-making. You must be able to state the opponents' case as well as they can themselves. Even if much that you oppose is wrong, negative tactics will not produce positive South Africanism. Perpetually, the enlightened electorate has been frustrated by the barrenness of party-politics and party techniques. Smuts realised only too well that he had sometimes followed party gain, as distinct from deeper principles. In retrospect, it is thus his holistic thought that is most important in our judgment of him.

4

Smuts's letters make it clear that he was aware of the great uncertainties that surround modern knowledge. Should we not therefore keep an open mind and allow time for intuitions to be demonstrated?

Aristarchos of Samos, in the third century B.C., put forward the theory that, contrary to the belief of his time, the earth went round the sun, not the sun round the earth. (See Farrington, *Greek Science, Thales to Aristotle* (Penguin) and Clagett, *Greek Science in Antiquity*.)

'Although we have no idea of the extent to which Aristarchus developed his system, it would not appear unreasonable to call him the Copernicus of antiquity, or perhaps it would be preferable to call Copernicus the Aristarchus of modern times.' (Clagett, *op. cit.*, p. 91).

In other words, an intuition that came in the third century B.C. had to wait until the sixteenth century A.D., before, in Copernicus's *De Revolutionibus*, it gradually gained general acceptance. Such is the slow progress of truth in a world of men with fixed ideas.

'Quantum mechanics,' said Einstein, 'is very impressive. The theory yields much, but it brings us no nearer to the secret of the Creator. I am convinced that He does not run the world by chance and by throwing dice.'

Others, such as Bohr and Born, held that modern experiment showed the world to be based on factors that *could* be classified as chance, and that two opposite tendencies, such as the particle and wave theories of light,

107

could exist at one and the same time. Schonland, in *The Atomists* (Oxford, 1969) takes up the theme: 'The final meaning of these and other startling results still remains to be found by workers with the great nuclear splitting machines. Whether they are learning the secrets of the universal, cosmic gambling operation, which Einstein refused to believe, remains to be discovered. Perhaps they will uncover only a vast and ingenious misunder-standing, inaugurated in ignorance by Galileo and Newton, and carried a stage further by the atomists of the nineteenth century.'

Different lines of development in Nature may con-stitute a kind of separate development. Bees and wasps keep their own lines of development, and have done so for centuries. The habits of bees as described by Vergil are still the habits we can recognise today. Certain lines do remain separate in spite of the ingenious theories of Darwin. The preservation of species, the regularity of Nature, the fulfilment of natural law (the *Foedera naturai* that impressed Lucretius), the accuracy of the seasons, the celestial phenomena, are these not mathematical demon-strations that 'God geometrises'? A definite and final statement of natural law is not possible. When authorities like Sir Basil Schonland speak of the possibility of 'a vast and ingenious misunderstanding inaugurated by Galileo and Newton,' we feel the world unstable beneath our feet.

5

The ease with which Smuts could associate with different kinds of people, whether scientists or children, especially in his later years, was based on real understanding and insight. He achieved a personal harmony, apart from political views and policies, that penetrated to the great leaders of the world, as well as to humbler friends. Among these were the Rain Queen, Princess Frederika of Greece, his own Isie (intellectually as well as personally), Alice Clark, Margaret Gillett, Emily Hobhouse, Gilbert Murray, Olive Schreiner, Louis Botha, Cecil John Rhodes, Winston Churchill, Jan Hofmeyr and his famous forebear Onze Jan, President Kruger, President Wilson and many others.

As a South African, he was a natural aristocrat, yet a man of the people; an intellectual giant, yet a son of the soil; an interpreter of Nature, yet a man who understood the simplest of human beings. He stood for 'South Africa first' but not 'South Africa alone'. His cause was a great one, and it is surely worthy of remembrance.

'In mind we reach the most significant factor in the universe, the supreme organ which controls all other structures and mechanisms. Mind is not yet the master, but it is the key in the hands of the master, Personality. It unlocks the door and releases the new-born spirit from the bonds and shackles and dungeons of natural necessity. It is the supreme system of control, and it holds the secret of freedom. Through the opened door, and the mists which still dim the eyes of the emergent spirit, it points to the great vistas of knowledge. Mind is the eye with which the universe beholds itself and knows itself divine.' (*Holism and Evolution*, Chap. IX, p. 238).

SELECT BIBLIOGRAPHY

ARMSTRONG, H. C.
    Grey steel: J. C. Smuts, a study in arrogance.
    Penguin, 1939.

BUCHAN, John, *baron* Tweedsmuir
    Memory hold-the-door. London, Hodder & Stough-
    ton, 1940

CLAGETT, M.
    Greek science in antiquity. London, Abelard-
Schuman, 1957.

COWELL, F. R.
    Culture in private and public life. London, Thames
    & Hudson, 1959.

DIELS, H.
    Die fragmente der Vorsokratiker, griechisch und
    deutsch. 6 verb. Aufl. hrsg. von Walther Kranz.
    Berlin, Weidmann, 1951. 3 v.

FARRINGTON, B.
    Greek science: its meaning for us. Penguin, 1953.

HANCOCK, (*Sir*) W. Keith
    Smuts. Cambridge university press, 1962–68. 2 v.
    v. 1: The sanguine years, 1870–1919.
    v. 2: The fields of force, 1919–1950.

HANCOCK, (*Sir*) W. Keith *and* Van der Poel, J. *ed.*
    Selections from the Smuts papers. Cambridge
    university press, 1966– vs. I–IV.

HOYLE, F.

. Man and materialism. London, Allen & Unwin, 1957.

JACKS, L. P.

The education of the whole man. London, University of London press, 1931.

JACOBI, J.

The psychology of Jung: an introduction . . . London, Kegan Paul, 1942.

LESKY, A.

A history of Greek literature. London, Methuen, 1966.

LOUW, A. M.

Die groot gryse. Kaapstad, Tafelberg, 1968.

MARAIS, J. S.

The fall of Kruger's republic. Oxford, Clarendon, 1961.

MILLIN, S. G.

General Smuts. London, Faber, 1936. 2 v.

PEAKE, A. S. *ed.*

Peake's Commentary on the Bible. London, Nelson, 1962.

ROSS, *Sir* William David

Aristotle. 5th ed. London, Methuen, repr. 1964.

SCHONLAND, *Sir* Basil

The atomists (1805–1933). Oxford, Clarendon, 1968.

SMUTS, J. C.

A century of wrong, London, Review of reviews, [1900].